simple
glass seed beading

simple
glass seed beading

Dorothy Wood

David & Charles

introduction

There is no doubt about it; seed beading is a fun and potentially addictive craft. These tiny beads, which come in such a myriad of colours and finishes, can be used in lots of different ways to make some really wonderful things. If this is your first foray into the world of beads, there will be new techniques to learn - although you may find that you already have many of the skills required to become a successful beader. The book is designed to inspire as well as instruct and so that you don't feel too restricted, the beads are simply described by size and colour on the project pages. You can enjoy looking for similar beads in your local bead shop or even try a different colour scheme to create some truly unique pieces. But don't despair: for those lacking the confidence to branch out on their own straight away, the exact beads used are listed at the back of the book on page 110.

The bead projects are divided into five groups, each using a different set of skills: bead loom work, needle weaving, fringes and tassels, bead embroidery and wirework. You may like to start with something you're familiar with or take the plunge and learn a completely new technique.

Although the projects all have simple step-by-step instructions, it is worth reading through the techniques section beginning on page 14, where you will find lots of tips and helpful advice. There are also clear instructions for some of the more common bead techniques used in the book, such as how to set up and use a bead loom and the basic needle weaving stitches.

Whatever your level of expertise there are plenty of projects to inspire and delight. Those new to the craft should begin with something simple, like the friendship bracelet and then work through the book, making lovely things and learning new skills as they go. Experienced beaders on the other hand can use the book as a source of ideas, choosing wonderful colours and textures to tailor the projects to suit their own taste.

materials and equipment

Beading requires very little specialist equipment - in fact all you need to begin is a needle and thread. Although it is possible to use any fine needle and thread, proper beading needles and thread will start you off in the right way and prevent problems arising later. All materials and equipment used in the book are readily available from craft or jewellery suppliers. If you don't have a local shop, check the supplier's list at the back of the book to find companies who operate a mail-order system or have web sites.

Needles

Beading needles are longer than normal sewing needles with a flat eye that can pass through the small holes in seed beads. The two most common sizes are 10 and 13. Size 10 is a good standard needle, but if you are going to pass the needle through a bead several times, you will need the finer size 13. Because they are so long and thin, beading needles can bend or break easily so make sure you have a good supply.

Thread

Polyester sewing thread is ideal for couching or embroidery techniques but a specialist beading thread is more suitable for all other beading techniques. Nymo thread is a strong, flat, nylon thread available in a range of sizes. The standard size for seed beads is D and the finer size B is ideal when passing the thread through a bead several times. Both thicknesses are available in a range of colours that can be matched to your beads. Cord threads are more suitable for making fringes and tassels as they allow the beads to swing attractively.

Thread conditioners

Thread conditioners strengthen and protect thread and make it less prone to tangling. It is not always necessary to condition threads when working with seed beads, but bugle and hex beads have sharp edges so condition your threads when using these. Run your thread through the conditioner, avoiding the needle area, and then pull the thread back through between your finger and thumb to remove any excess conditioner and smooth the thread.

Scissors

A sharp pair of embroidery scissors is useful for cutting thread to length and snipping off threads close to the beadwork. Use larger dressmaking scissors for cutting fabric.

Bead mats

Use a bead mat to spread the beads out while you work, so you can discard any misshapen ones and pick the beads up easily on the needle. To make one, cut a piece of chamois leather, or glue a square of velvet to card. The close pile on these materials prevents the beads from rolling away as you pick them up.

Jewellery findings

Choose the method of fastening your jewellery before you begin beading so that you leave enough thread to attach the findings or to make a bead fastening. Clasps and ear wires are readily available from bead suppliers. More unusual fastenings are available by mail order. Use wood beads to make small beaded toggles and tassle heads.

Embroidery hoop

An embroidery hoop or frame keeps the fabric taut while you embroider with beads and prevents puckering.

Fabric markers

Use a vanishing ink pen to mark out motifs on fabric. The ink marks will disappear after a few hours.

Wire

Wire is used in beadwork when the beads have to hold a particular shape or if the wire is part of the decorative effect. Jewellery wire and coloured enamel wire are available in a wide range of colours and thicknesses, from 0.2mm (36swg) to 1.2mm (18swg). 0.4mm (27swg) wire is ideal for stringing size 11 seed beads. Standard wire gauge (swg or SWG) is a UK scale of wire thickness.

Pliers and wire cutters

Bend wire with flat-nosed pliers or use them to pull the needle through a bead that is tightly packed with thread. Flat-nosed pliers are also useful if you have threaded too many beads on to your thread. To avoid taking off all the beads from the thread, simply grasp the unwanted

bead in the tip of the pliers and squeeze until it breaks. Cover your eyes, as the bead will shatter into tiny glass shards.

Round-nosed pliers are used to bend wire to make jump rings in a range of sizes. You can cut wire with most pliers, but it is much easier to cut close to the beadwork with wire cutters.

Bead looms

There are several different bead looms available, some are wooden and others have a stiff wire frame. Basic looms are suitable for making bead bands up to 6cm (2½in) wide, although the wire spring restricts the number of warp threads that can be strung on the loom. For weaving bands of beads wider than 30–35 beads, you will need to buy or make a wider loom with a longer spring or coil.

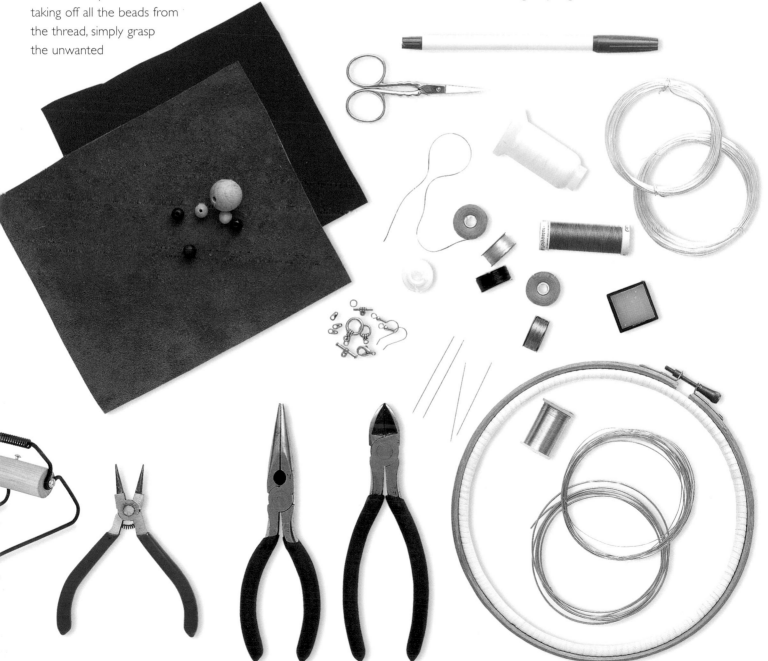

beads

At first sight all the beads in a bead shop look the same, but close inspection reveals a wide variety of shapes and sizes. When buying beads from a catalogue or on the web it helps to know the different types of beads and the names of the different finishes, as it is not always obvious what the beads actually look like from the photograph.

Seed beads are round, donut-shaped beads ranging in size from 5 to 15. Larger seed beads are known as **pony** beads and the smaller ones as **petites**. The most common sized seed beads are size 11 or 12.

Hex beads are cylindrical beads made from a six-sided glass cane. They are like a squat bugle bead and are useful for creating texture.

Cylinder beads, also known by their trade names **Delicas**, **Antiques** and **Magnificas**, are precision-milled tubular beads. They are ideal for needle and loom weaving as the beads sit next to one another and create an even bead fabric. They have a large hole enabling you to pass a needle and thread through each bead several times.

Bugle beads are made in a similar way to seed beads. The glass canes are cut to a variety of lengths from 2–30mm (1/16–1 1/4in). The most common sizes are 4mm (3/16in), 6mm (1/4in), 9mm (3/16in) and 15mm (5/8in). Twisted bugle beads are made from five- or six-sided tubes that have been twisted while the glass is still hot.

bead finishes

Beads often have two or more different descriptive words that explain exactly what the bead looks like. For example 'SL purple AB' is a silver-lined purple bead with an iridescent, rainbow effect on the surface (AB meaning aurora borealis). It is like a code system – once you know the code you can tell exactly what you are buying (see facing page, choosing and buying beads.) The combinations of these different finishes produce a huge variety of different beads.

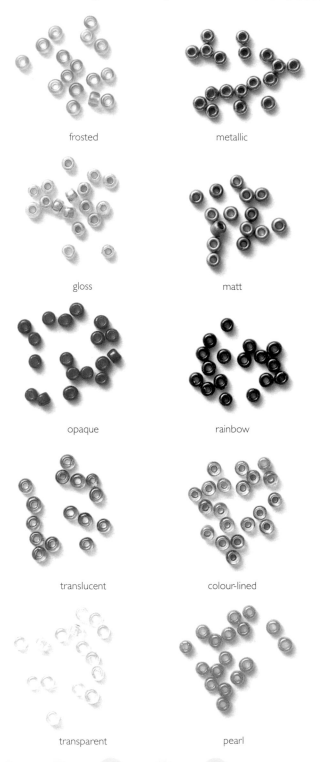

frosted

metallic

gloss

matt

opaque

rainbow

translucent

colour-lined

transparent

pearl

Transparent beads are clear or coloured glass that allow the light to pass through. Using a dark-coloured thread can alter the bead colour. **Opaque** beads are solid colour beads that don't allow any light to pass through. **Translucent** beads are in between transparent and opaque and are also known variously as greasy, opal and satin. **Greasy** beads are made from cloudy-looking glass while **opal** beads are slightly more transparent. **Satin** beads have tiny bubbles in the glass, which give the bead a directional sheen.

Gloss beads are very shiny, like glass. **Matt** beads are opaque beads that have been tumbled or dipped in acid to give them a dull, flat surface. **Frosted** beads are clear or translucent beads, which have been treated in a similar way.

Lustre beads have a transparent coating, either coloured or clear, that gives the beads a subtle shine. **Ceylon** beads have a milky, pearlized lustre.

Colour-lined (CL) beads have the hole in the bead lined with another colour. The beads can be clear or coloured. **Silver-lined** (SL) beads have the hole in the bead lined with silver and look very sparkly. These beads can be bleached to remove the silver lining leaving a more subtle finish.

Metallic beads include any bead that looks metallic. The finish can be painted on or in the case of galvanized beads the finish is electroplated to the surface of the bead. Beads with painted metallic finishes cannot be washed. **Iris** or **rainbow** beads have been treated with metal salts to create a coating that resembles an oil slick. They are often made from dark or black opaque beads and are also known as aurora borealis (AB) beads.

choosing and buying beads

It has never been easier to buy beads because even if you don't have a bead shop nearby there are lots of mail order and internet companies to choose from. The beads are usually clearly illustrated, with precise details of their size, colour and finish. Look at the suppliers listed on page 111 for some useful addresses to get you started stocking up on your own supply of beads.

The quality of seed beads available on the market varies, and you generally get what you pay for. The finest quality beads come from Japan, and this is often marked on the packet. When needle weaving or loom weaving it is essential to buy good quality beads that are of an even size, although it is fine to use less expensive beads for netting, fringing and coiling on wire.

Make use of your knowledge of the different types of beads when choosing them for your projects. Even if the beadwork appears to be all one colour, pick a selection of beads with different finishes to give the beadwork interest and vitality. You can use any size of seed bead for the projects although best results will be achieved using the correct size and type of bead specified in the text. For a unique finish, choose your own colours but if you would rather buy the exact beads used in the projects, full details are listed on page 110.

Seed beads, cylinder beads and bugles are sold in a variety of packets, bags and tubes with no standard bead packet sizes. The packets or containers usually have the weight of beads marked, making it easier to decide how many packets you require. Some beads are sold in round weights such as 5g or 100g; others are sold with a particular number of beads and so have an odd weight such as 4.54g. Unfortunately the number of beads is not marked. Do check the weight of each different bead – some companies keep the bead quantity the same in each packet and vary the price, whereas others keep the price the same and alter the quantity.

Depending on the size or type of bead there are an average number of beads per gram so that it is fairly easy to work out what quantity of beads you need for a certain project. Use the chart here to help you work out how many beads you require.

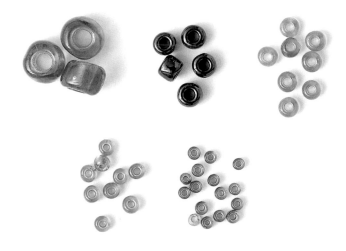

Type of bead	Size of bead	5g bag (approx.)
Pony bead	5	65
Seed bead	8	200
Seed bead	9	300
Seed bead	11	450
Seed bead	12	500
Petite bead	15	950
Cylinder bead	Delicas	800
Bugle bead	3mm	20
Bugle bead	7mm	150
Bugle bead	9mm	90
Bugle bead	15mm	55

techniques

If you are new to beadwork it is worth working through this section to learn the skills required for some of the projects. Although most of the projects have full instructions enabling you to work the project from the step-by-step instructions, this section has useful tips and diagrams as well as detailed instructions for using a bead loom, embroidering with beads and all the needle weaving stitches used in the book.

beginning a piece of beadwork

Work with as long a length of thread as you can comfortably sew with to reduce the number of joins – between 1–2m (1–2yd) is ideal. Nymo thread is easier to thread straight off the reel. If you are using a round thread such as quilting thread, flatten the end and trim at an angle before threading the needle. To prevent the thread from knotting, let the needle hang loose from time to time to unwind. If it does coil up and loop into a knot don't panic and pull the thread tight, simply put the needle into the loop and pull gently to one side to ease the knot out.

When needle weaving, a stop bead will stabilize the first row and prevent the beads from falling off. You can use the first bead in the row or use a bead in a different colour that can be removed at a later stage.

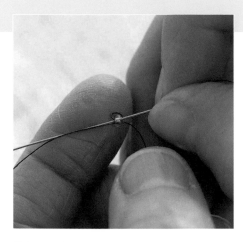

Pick up a bead and pass the needle back through it once or twice to anchor it. Leave a tail of at least 15cm (6in) for finishing off or adding a fastening.

joining on another thread

Don't work right to the end of a thread. Leave a tail of 15cm (6in) to make it easier to attach a new thread and weave the ends back into the work.

1 In closely packed beadwork, weave the new thread back and forward across the beadwork several times bringing the new thread out through the same bead as the old thread. At a later stage, weave the old thread through the new beadwork in the same way and trim off the ends.

2 When working nets or fringes, knot the two threads together using a reef knot (see facing page). Using a needle, manoeuvre the knot between two beads or to the edge of the work before tightening. Weave the ends into the work and trim close to the beads. A tiny drop of fray check liquid or clear nail varnish will secure the knot permanently.

knots used in beading

There are several simple knots used in beading to anchor threads or for tying off ends securely and it is worthwhile learning these knots so that your beadwork remains intact and fastenings firmly attached during use. For extra security use a cocktail stick to drop a tiny amount of fixative, such as clear nail polish or a fray check liquid, on the knots.

double half hitch

Use this knot to secure a thread in netting or fringes before feeding the end through several more beads and trimming the end.

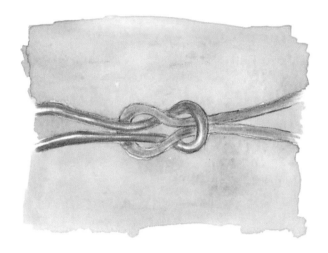

reef (square) knot

This is the basic knot for joining two threads of equal thickness. Feed each end back through several beads before trimming the ends.

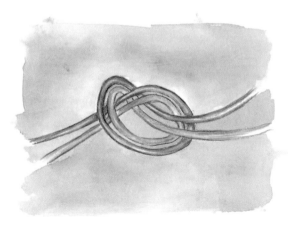

overhand knot

Use this knot to tie threads together before fitting on a bead loom or to join two threads together at the edge of a piece of work. The knot can be easily manoeuvred into position with a needle.

surgeon's knot

This knot is similar to a reef knot but each thread end is taken over and under twice. The knot is more secure than a reef knot and doesn't loosen while it is being tied.

bead loom weaving

Bead loom weaving is a quick method of producing flat bands of beading. The width of the band is only restricted by the width of the loom. Bead weaving on a loom produces a similar result to the square stitch in needle weaving. The beads are arranged in straight rows and so the design can be worked out on a square grid in the same way as cross stitch. There are two sets of threads on a bead loom. The warp threads run lengthways through the beadwork and are fitted to the loom. The weft threads are crossways threads, which carry the beads and are woven in with a beading needle.

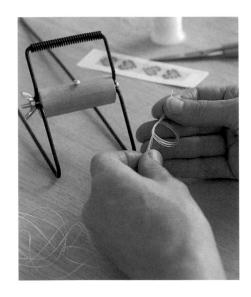  

1 Count the number of beads across the design and add one to find the number of warp threads required. Add 60cm (24in) to the finished length of the project for attaching the threads to the loom and finishing off. Cut the warp threads and tie an overhand knot (see page 15) at one end.

2 Split the bundle in two and loop the knot over the tack on the top roller. Loosen the wing nut and, holding the threads taut, wind the warp threads on to the roller, stopping when there is just enough thread to tie on to the other roller.

3 Hold the threads firmly and arrange along the top spring. Use a 'T' pin to sort one thread into each coil. Line the threads up across the bottom spring in the same way, so that they run parallel to one another and don't cross at any point.

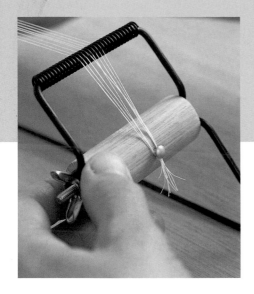

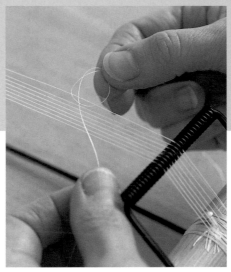

4 Tie an overhand knot and loop the knot over the tack on the bottom roller. Wind the rollers back until there is about 30cm (12in) on the bottom roller and tighten the wing nuts.

5 Thread a needle with a 2m (2¼yd) length of thread and tie to the left-hand side warp thread with an overhand knot leaving a 15cm (6in) tail. Beginning at the bottom, read the beadwork chart from right to left and pick up the required number of beads in the right order.

6 Hold the beads under the warp threads and push them up between the warp threads so that there is a thread either side of each bead.

7 Feed the needle back through the beads from left to right, making sure that the needle passes on top of the warp threads. If the needle goes below the warp thread the beads will not be secured.

8 Pick up the next row of beads according to the chart and repeat the process, passing the needle back through the beads above the warp threads. After the first few rows it will become much easier to work.

9 When you have about 13cm (5in) of thread left on the weft thread remove the needle and leave the thread hanging. Thread a new length of thread and feed through five or six beads, leaving a 13cm (5in) tail hanging below the beadwork. Both ends can be woven in later.

10 To finish the beadwork, weave the weft thread, without any beads on it, back and forward across the top of the beads to create a narrow fabric band. Roll the beadwork to the other end. Now attach another length of thread and weave this thread to create a narrow band of fabric at the beginning of the beadwork.

11 Lift the beadwork off the loom. Tie pairs of warp threads together using a surgeon's knot (see page 15). Take the thread ends left over right, twice, and then right over left, twice, and pull tight.

12 Weave the ends of the thread into the beadwork for at least five beads and then double back for at least five beads. Trim the ends close to the beadwork on the reverse side and then trim the warp threads at each end to 6mm (¼in).

needle weaving

Needle weaving is a way of stitching beads together to create a flat or tubular beaded fabric. There are lots of different stitches that can be used, each with distinct characteristics that determine the finished look and feel of the beadwork. The stitches may appear to be similar in samples but are not readily interchangeable, as their different characteristics become evident in larger pieces. Square stitch, ladder stitch, brick stitch, peyote stitch and chain stitch are described below.

ladder stitch

This simple stitch is often used to make the base for brick stitch. It is usually worked with bugle beads but seed beads can also be used.

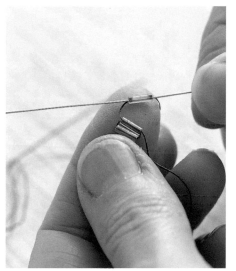
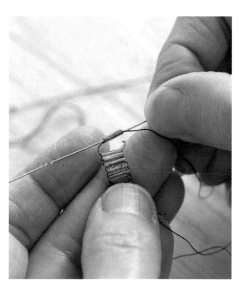

1 Cut a 2m (2¼yd) length of thread and thread a needle on to each end. Pick up two bugle beads and let them drop down to the middle of the thread. Now put the other needle through the second bead in the opposite direction.

2 Pull the threads tight. Pick up another bead with one needle and put the other needle through the bead in the opposite direction.

3 Continue adding beads in the same way until the band is the length you require. To make the band into a tube, pass each needle through the first bead again and pull tight.

square stitch

Beads worked in square stitch look similar to beads woven on a loom. The needle passes through each bead several times and so you may need to use a size 13 needle and a fine thread in a toning colour. Square stitch has a wonderful draping quality and is ideal for bracelets.

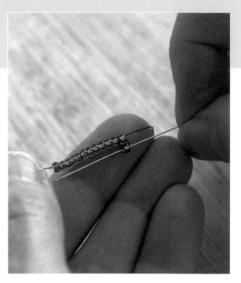

1 Pick up the required number of beads for the first row. For the second row, pick up a bead and pass the needle back through the last bead on the first row.

2 Pass the needle through the first bead on the second row again and back through the bead just added. The bead should be suspended below the first row.

3 Pick up a second bead and take the needle back through the second last bead on the previous row. Continue working along the row adding on one bead at a time.

4 To strengthen the fabric, at the end of the row go back through the previous row and the one just worked, ready to begin the next row.

brick stitch

Brick stitch is one of the easiest stitches to work and is so called because it looks like a brick wall. The stitch is flexible crossways but rather stiff lengthways and can be worked flat or in a tube. It is often used to make tiny bags, such as the amulet purse (see page 46).

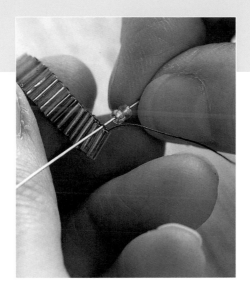

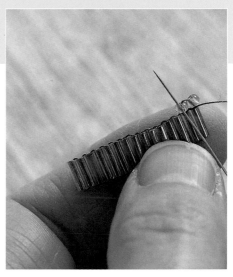

1 Make the foundation row the required length in ladder stitch (see page 19), using either seed beads or bugle beads. For the first row of brick stitch, pick up two beads and pass the needle under the first loop of thread joining the foundation row of beads.

2 Pass the needle back through the second bead you picked up. Pick up another bead. Pass the needle under the next loop and back through the bead again. Continue adding one bead at a time in this way to the end of the row.

3 Turn the beading round and pick up two beads to begin the next row. Repeat steps 2 and 3 until the beadwork is the size that you require.

4 To work in a tube, make a foundation tube with ladder stitch. At the beginning of each row pick up two beads and at the end of the row join the beads together and bring the thread out ready to begin the next row.

peyote stitch

Peyote stitch is a versatile stitch that can be worked flat or in a tube. It is easiest to work with an even number of beads in each row. Peyote stitch is ideal for bags with a flap, as the fabric is very flexible along its length.

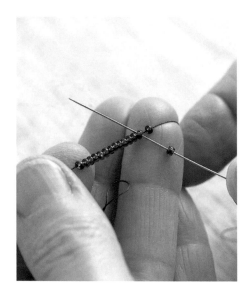

1 Pick up a bead and anchor it by taking the needle back through it again leaving a 15cm (6in) tail. Pick up enough beads to give the required width for the first row, ending up with an even number. Pick up a bead and, missing the last bead on the first row, pass the needle through the next bead.

2 Pick up another bead, miss a bead on the first row and pass the needle through the next bead. Continue to the end of the row missing every second bead.

3 In subsequent rows the beads are in a more obvious zigzag pattern. Work back and forward in the same way, picking up one bead at a time and passing the needle through the next 'dropped down' bead.

chain stitch

Chain stitch is an ideal stitch for making straps and can be embellished to make more ornate bracelets and necklaces. The number of beads can be varied in each chain to create different effects.

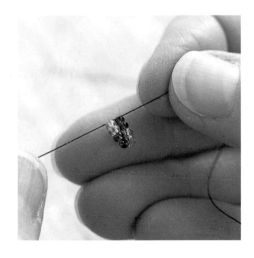

1 Pick up two light beads, two dark beads, two light beads and two dark beads. Tie the beads into a circle using a reef knot (see page 15), leaving a 15cm (6in) tail.

2 Pass the needle back through two dark, two light and two dark beads. Pick up two light, two dark and two light beads and put the needle back through the top two dark beads on the previous chain.

3 Pass the needle through the first two light and two dark beads just added, ready to add the next chain. Continue adding six beads at a time until the chain is the length required.

joining pieces of beadwork

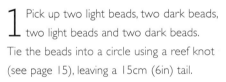

From time to time it is necessary to make a seam and join two pieces of beadwork. In beadwork it is possible to make an invisible join. Square stitch and peyote stitch both have flat sides and can be butted together. Pass the needle and thread through one bead at a time alternating from side to side to join the seam.

To join pieces of brick stitch, it is necessary to slot the two pieces together using the beads jutting out in the alternate rows as shown.

Put the needle through the jutting-out bead on one side. Take it through the jutting-out bead on the opposite side and pull tight. Continue working down the seam.

bead embroidery

Bead embroidery transforms everyday objects into luxury items. Beads can be attached individually, in groups or in rows to most fabrics, and two stitches, backstitch and couching, are described below.

preparing to embroider

If the fabric is flimsy it needs to be supported in a hoop or frame while working so that the beadwork does not scrunch up. If possible use a backing fabric to anchor any threads on the reverse side. Use a double length of sewing thread in the needle or one strand of a beading thread such as Nymo.

1 Cut the fabric and any backing fabric at least 5cm (2in) larger all round than the finished piece. Fit the fabric into an embroidery hoop or on to a rotary frame.

2 Take two tiny backstitches on the reverse side and bring the needle out on the right side where you want the beadwork to begin. You are now ready to start your bead embroidery.

backstitch

Backstitch is a useful stitch in bead embroidery as it can be used to add individual beads or several at a time. Only pick up one or two beads to follow a curved line but pick up more the straighter the line, taking the needle back through the last bead each time.

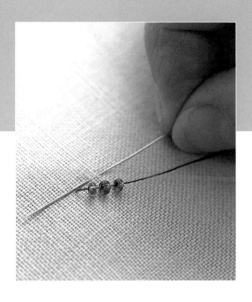

1 Pick up three beads and drop them down to where the thread emerges. Put the needle back into the fabric at the end of the three beads. Take a small backstitch and bring the needle out between the last two beads.

2 Put the needle back through the last bead and then pick up another three beads ready to begin again.

couching

Couching is used to apply a string of beads to fabric in a straight line or curve. You need to use two needles on separate lengths of thread - one beading needle and one sewing needle.

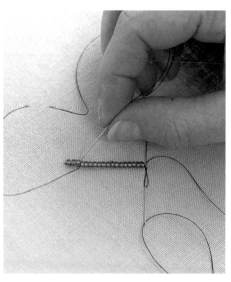

1 Bring the beading needle out where you want the beadwork to begin. Pick up sufficient beads to complete the line. If the beads are being couched in a straight line, put the beading needle in the fabric and wrap the thread around to hold the beads taut.

2 Bring the second thread out between the first and second beads. Take the thread over the bead string and back through the fabric. Work down the bead strand, stitching between every bead or in groups of three or four. At the end take both threads to the reverse side and secure them.

the projects

The beauty of seed beads is that they are so versatile - tiny pieces of glass that can be put together in so many different ways to create wonderful things. As with any craft there are techniques to be learnt but once these skills have been perfected the possibilities are endless.

In this book there are projects for the home, some beautiful pieces of jewellery and a few personal items that have been trimmed with beads to make them quite unique. Many of the projects are ideal for gifts; although they are all so beautiful I'm sure you'll be reluctant to give away anything you make! A bracelet only takes a few hours and can be made in any colour you choose or you could make a set of rose-scented sachets and decorate them with pretty beads. For a more substantial gift, add a net fringe to a beautiful devoré scarf or make a tiny amulet purse to give to your best friend. To finish off, why not make a beaded card to send with your gift or decorate a pretty gift bag with a few wire flowers.

Beads can be used to embellish all sorts of items in the home - add a sparkly fringe to a lampshade, wrap a beaded wire around plain glass candlesticks or trim a trinket box with iridescent beads. Some items around the home can be made almost entirely of beads, such as an exquisite bead tassel to hang from a wardrobe key, a delightful bead frame for your favourite photograph, or a set of coiled wire coasters for the dining room.

Finally, there are beautiful things to make just for you. Embroider a silk cover for a notebook or address book, make a natural linen rucksack embroidered with classic matt beads or step out in style in a pair of silk mules decorated with exquisite paisley motifs.

friendship bracelet

Loom weaving is a quick
and easy way of creating
flat bands of beading
and this simple bracelet
is the ideal first bead
loom project. It is made
using tiny tubular beads
called Delicas, which
are very even and lock
together tightly to make
a smooth bead fabric.
It has been cleverly
designed with fastenings
made entirely of beads
and so no clasps or
hooks are required.
As the name implies,
these pretty bracelets
are intended to be given
as tokens of friendship.
If you have an extra
special friend, why not
add a delicate picot
edging down either side
of the bracelet to
finish it off?

friendship bracelet

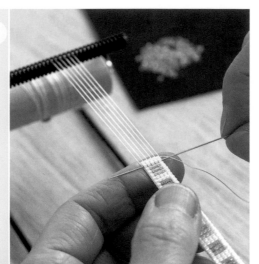

you will need

- bead loom
- beading needle
- white Nymo thread
- 2g white delicas
- 1g lime delicas
- 1g aqua delicas
- 1g bright blue delicas
- scissors

1 Set up the bead loom with six 76cm (30in) long white Nymo threads (see bead loom weaving, page 16). To calculate the length of the bracelet, measure the circumference of your wrist and take off 1cm (½in) for the fastening. Following the beadwork chart on page 108, work the bead design to this length ending with two white rows. Put the needle back through the second last row of beads.

2 Bring the needle out between the first two beads on the last row. Pick up three aqua delicas and fit under the centre four threads. Take the needle back through the beads. Work another two rows avoiding the outside threads.

try this

If you prefer, you could leave the bracelet without the picot edging and make a short length of beadwork to create a pretty matching ring.

3 Wind the loom back to the other end of the bracelet and add a block of nine aqua delicas to that end as well. Take the beadwork off the loom. Sew the thread ends back into the bracelet leaving one thread next to the centre aqua bead at each end.

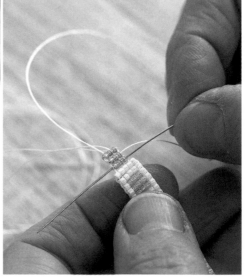

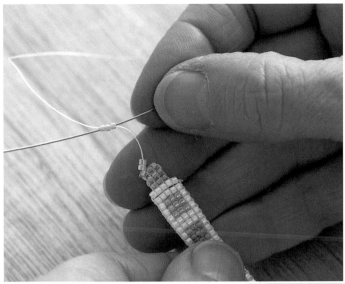

4 To make a toggle pick up five lime beads and put the needle back through the last three to make a circle. Pick up a bead and put the needle through the centre of the circle. Keep adding beads one at time, putting the needle through the cluster until you make a 6mm (¼in) toggle.

tip

Tie a double half hitch knot (see page 15) between two beads before sewing the thread ends of the loop into the bracelet to make it extra secure.

5 At the other end of the bracelet pick up enough lime delicas to make a loop that will pass over the toggle snugly. Put the needle back through the other side of the centre aqua bead and then back through the loop before securing the end in the bracelet.

6 To add a picot edge, attach a thread at one end of the bracelet and bring it out at the edge of the bracelet opposite the centre lime delica. Pick up three lime delicas and put the needle through the bracelet, bringing it out on the other side.

7 Pick up another three beads and put the needle back through the first two in the bracelet. Feed the needle down to the next coloured centre bead and then out to the edge. Make a picot on either side and continue down the bracelet adding matching picots either side of each square. Secure the end of the thread in the bracelet to finish.

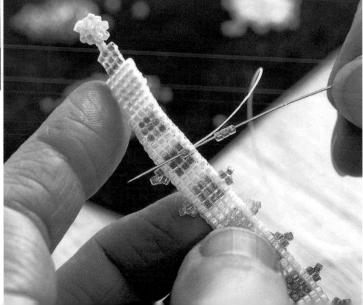

bead frame

Inspired by the wonderful patterns on a zebra's coat and designed using neutral colours reminiscent of the Sahara Desert, this unusual frame is created using more than 8,000 beads. Using a wide bead loom, it is surprisingly quick to weave. The beadwork is woven in strips which are then sewn together invisibly before being made into a picture frame. The beads used to make the frame are cylinders, also known as Delicas, Magnificas or Antiques. Unlike seed beads, which are donut-shaped, cylinder beads are short tubes that slot together to make a more even, flat bead fabric.

bead frame

you will need

- wide bead loom
- beige Nymo thread
- beading needle
- 10g dark gold delicas
- 25g dark cream delicas
- 30g rose/green metallic delicas
- masking tape
- 6mm (¼in) wide double-sided tape
- mount board
- craft knife
- cutting mat
- spray adhesive

1 Fit thirty-four 1.25m (49in) lengths of thread into the bead loom (see bead loom weaving, page 16). Following the beadwork chart on page 106, weave both side panels on these threads, leaving a 30cm (12in) gap between panels. Weave a thread panel at both ends of each panel before lifting off the loom. Now weave the top and bottom panels on fifty-one 1m (1yd) lengths of thread leaving a 30cm (12in) gap between the panels. Weave a thread panel at both ends of each panel before lifting off the loom. Sew in any side threads. Secure the bead panels to the work surface with masking tape and tie the thread ends together in pairs using a surgeon's knot (see page 15).

tip

If you find that you have missed one of the warp threads after lifting the beadwork off the loom, thread the beading needle and weave another length of thread in to correct the error.

2 Stick a piece of double-sided tape along the top and bottom edges of each bead panel on the reverse side. Fold the threads back on to the double-sided tape and trim the threads to 6mm (¼in).

3 Lay the bead panels out on a flat surface. Weave a thread into one of the side panels bringing it out in the inside corner. Feed the needle through the first three beads in the adjacent panel.

4 Take the needle back through the three beads in the next row and then through the first three beads in the adjacent panel. Work along the seam, sewing back and forward through the beads to join the seam.

5 Join all four seams in the same way. Measure the height and width of the bead panel leaving one row of beads all round. Cut two pieces of mount board that size.

6 Measure the size of the aperture and, using a sharp craft knife and cutting mat, cut a window in one of the pieces of mount board. Stick the bead frame to this piece of board using spray adhesive. Now stick double-sided tape down the sides and along the bottom of the aperture piece of mount board and stick it on top of the second piece.

try this

For a more substantial frame, cover each piece of mount board in fabric and stitch the bead panel in position rather than using glue.

7 To make a stand, cut a 5 x 15cm (2 x 6in) piece of mount board and score a line 5cm (2in) from one end. Apply double-sided tape above the score line and stick the stand on the back of the frame. Place your photo in the frame through the top opening.

bead frame 35

trinket box

Three different bead techniques are combined to make this beautiful trinket box. The rim is covered with a stunning piece of bead loom weaving, the padded lid is decorated with hand embroidered beads and the box is finished off with an exquisite, three-dimensional beaded blackberry. Use a soft fabric such as georgette that drapes well to cover the outside of the box. The inside of the box can be as luxurious or plain as you like. Cover the inside raw edge with a strip of co-ordinating ribbon or cut a strip of card to fit inside and cover this with plain or padded fabric.

trinket box

you will need

- bead loom
- petrol blue Nymo thread
- beading needle
- 6g iridescent pale aqua seed beads
- 5g iridescent blue rainbow seed beads
- 6g iridescent green/blue iris seed beads
- 3g deep blue seed beads
- 3g blue/green seed beads
- 3g dark olive green seed beads
- 3g pink seed beads
- scissors
- circular papier mâché box 12cm (4¾in) diameter
- 1.25cm (½in) wide double-sided tape
- 30cm (12in) lilac georgette
- 50g (2oz) wadding (batting)
- 15cm (6in) diameter circle of organdie
- 7mm (⁵⁄₁₆in) wooden bead
- dressmaker's pin
- spray adhesive
- thin card

1 Fit fourteen 1m (39in) lengths of petrol blue Nymo thread into the loom, (see bead loom weaving, page 16). Work the bead design following the chart on page 108. You will need four repeats plus one extra diamond to fit this size of box. Take the beading off the loom and check the length against the box rim. Allow 6mm (¼in) for the fabric covering and remove a row or two of beads if required. Put the beadwork back on the loom and weave the fabric ends.

2 Stick double-sided tape around the inside and outside of the lid rim. Cut a 5 x 40cm (2 x 15¾in) strip of georgette and stick it halfway down the rim on the outside. Fold over the raw edge of the overlap and use double-sided tape to secure. Smooth the strip of fabric over to the inside of the lid.

3 Cut six circles of wadding (batting) the same size as the lid. Cut another slightly larger and two smaller circles. Stick another piece of double-sided tape around the rim of the lid. Pile the wadding (batting) on top of the lid beginning with the smallest circle and finishing with the largest one.

4 Position the organdie over the wadding (batting) and stretch it gently on to the double-sided tape. Adjust the organdie until the top is a smooth dome and trim any excess fabric.

tip

Don't be tempted to skip step 4. Organdie is a fine, closely woven fabric that gives a superior finish to the padding on the box lid. Softer dress fabric does not give a smooth result.

5 Stick more double-sided tape around the rim of the lid. Stretch a 15cm (6in) diameter circle of georgette on to the double-sided tape and trim off the excess fabric. Tie off the threads on the bead strip and fold the woven fabric under. Stick the bead strip around the rim, butting the ends together.

6 Using the point of a pair of embroidery scissors, make a hole in the centre of the lid from the inside. Tie a knot in the end of a length of Nymo thread and feed it through the hole. Leaving a 1cm (½in) circle in the centre clear of beads, begin to stitch green/blue iris beads in the middle of the lid. Work out from the centre, spacing the beads out further and using progressively lighter iridescent beads.

7 To make the blackberry, thread the beading needle and pick up the wooden bead, tying the thread to it, leaving a 10cm (4in) tail. Cover the bead with rows of 8 dark olive green seed beads. Begin to fill the gaps with some of the other colour beads, threading the needle under the dark olive green rows.

8 Keep adding beads used in the design until the wooden bead resembles a blackberry. Feed the thread ends through the centre of the lid and out of the hole on the reverse side.

9 From inside, lay an ordinary dressmaker's pin across the hole. Push down on the blackberry to sink it into the wadding (batting) and tie the threads across the pin using a surgeon's knot (see page 15). The pin stays in place.

10 Cut a strip of georgette fabric 3cm (1¼in) deeper than the box base and long enough to wrap around it. Stick double-sided tape on the inside of the rim and around the base. Stick the fabric around the box and then tuck the excess inside. Stretch the fabric gently on to the base of the box.

11 Cut two circles of thin card the same size as the base of the box and trim one slightly smaller. Spray adhesive on one side of each circle and stick to a piece of georgette. Trim the fabric to 1cm (½in) and snip into the card all round. Spray with adhesive and stretch the fabric on to the reverse side.

try this

Create an attractive card to match the trinket box by weaving a small square, using the chart on page 108. Weave the fabric border at each end and use double sided tape to stick the beadwork inside the aperture.

12 Stick the larger covered circle inside the lid and the smaller circle on to the base of the box. To finish the inside of the box simply cover the raw fabric edge with a piece of co-ordinating ribbon.

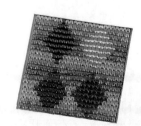

spiral bracelets

Needle weaving, described fully on page 19, is perfect for creating jewellery so why not add a finishing touch to your favourite outfit with this set of matching bracelets? Although they look very delicate, these spiral bracelets are made with a strong beading stitch that is unlikely to break. You can use any beads you like to make the bracelets but it is better to choose contrasting colours or textures for the inside and outside beads so that the spiral is quite obvious. To make a chunkier bracelet, use larger beads on the outside of the spiral and finish off with a heavier toggle fastening.

spiral bracelets

you will need

- white Nymo thread
- beading needle
- 2g grass green seed beads
- 3g mint green seed beads
- 3g aqua size 8 seed beads
- scissors
- toggle fastening

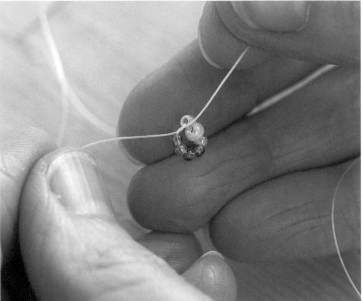

1 Thread the beading needle with a 2m (2¼yd) length of white Nymo thread. Pick up 4 grass green beads, then 1 mint green bead, 1 aqua bead and another mint green bead. Tie the beads into a circle, leaving a 15cm (6in) tail.

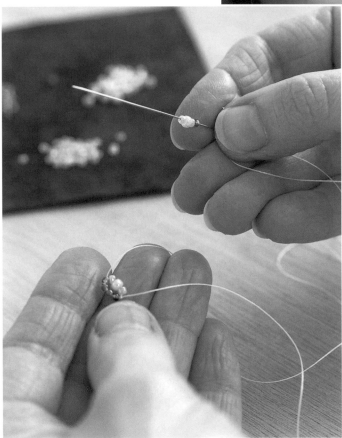

2 Pass the needle through the 4 grass green beads. Pick up 1 grass green bead, 1 mint green, 1 aqua and another mint green. Let the beads drop down to the work.

tip

Use a fine size 13 beading needle and size 'b' thread to make the bracelet so that you are able to take the needle and thread through some of the beads several times.

try this

Make a matching bracelet using the more unusual hex beads to create a distinct pattern that looks like a helter-skelter. Create a different effect by using dark beads on the outside and pale beads on the inside.

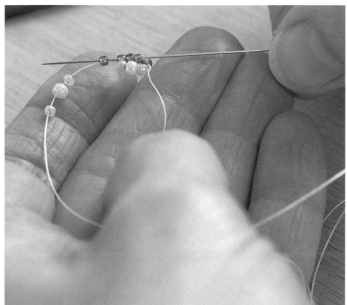

3 Pass the needle back through the last three grass green beads and the one just added. Pull the thread tight and position the beads next to the previous group of mint green/aqua beads.

4 Pick up 1 grass green bead, 1 mint green, 1 aqua and 1 mint green. Let the beads drop down to the work. Repeat steps 3 and 4. The spiral will only become obvious when you have made about eight repetitions.

5 Continue adding beads until the spiral is the length required, approximately 17cm (6¾in). Oversew the two halves of the toggle fastening to the ends of the bracelet. Feed the needle back down through 3 or 4 beads, tie a double half hitch knot and feed the needle through another 3 or 4 beads. Trim the thread close to the beads.

amulet purse

An amulet is a charm, something worn as protection from misfortune or evil spirits. Traditionally, these delightful purses were hung around the neck with the charm tucked safely inside. Nowadays an amulet purse has a more decorative purpose and is worn as a rather unusual necklace. It is worked in brick stitch from a chart, with the design repeated twice so that the back and front are identical. The purse is rather tiny and doesn't hold very much, but it could still protect you from misfortune: keep a little money folded up inside and you should get home safely!

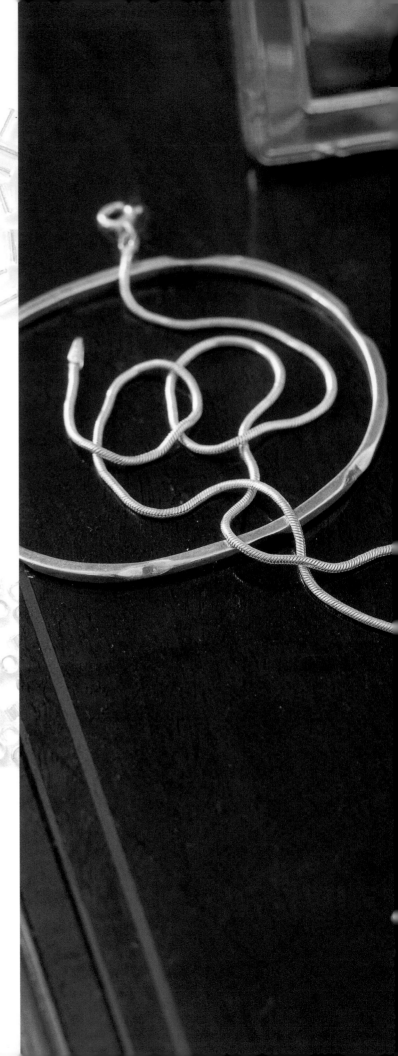

amulet purse

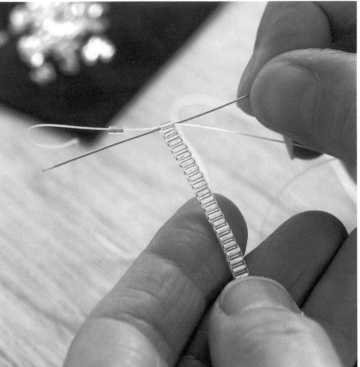

1 Thread a long length of white Nymo thread with a beading needle at each end. Work ladder stitch (see page 19) using the bugle beads until there are 50 beads and then join the strip into a circle.

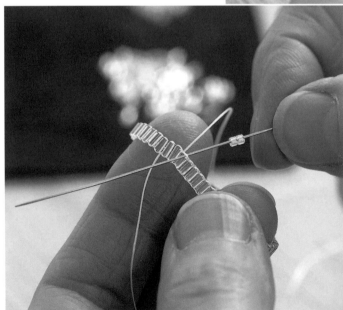

2 Working in brick stitch (see page 21) follow the chart on page 107, starting on Row 1. Pick up two light pink delicas and put the needle through the first loop and back through the second bead threaded. Continue working brick stitch, repeating the chart twice until you reach the first bead again.

3 Stitch these two beads together and then begin the next row as in step 2. Keep following the chart, working tubular brick stitch until you complete Row 30. Now fold the purse in half so that the hearts are in the centre.

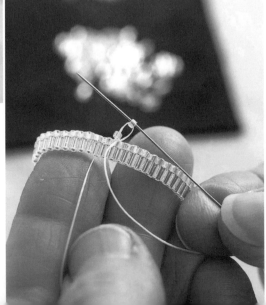

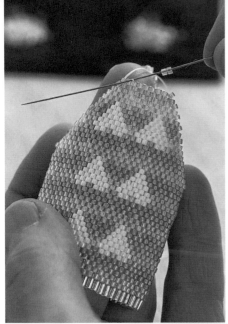

4 From now on you will not be stitching a tube but should continue working brick stitch one side at a time, decreasing the beads at each edge, as shown on the chart. To decrease, pick up two beads as usual but put the needle through the second loop from the edge and work across the row as normal. Now join on a thread on the other side of the amulet and complete the back of the purse in the same way. Once both sides are complete, stitch the side seams together invisibly (see page 23).

(see page 23).

try this

Instead of a tassel you could add a fringe to the bottom edge of the purse. Join on a thread at one side of the purse and pick up 20 seed beads and 2 bugles. Take the needle back through the seed beads and bring it out ready to start the next fringe strand.

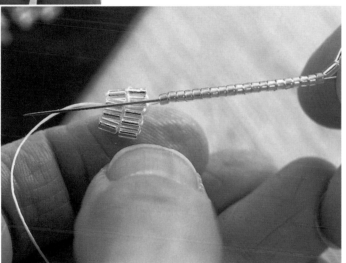

5 Make an eight-bugle strip in ladder stitch and join into a tube. Add a second row of bugles using brick stitch. To make a tassel string, cut a 2m (2¼yd) length of cord thread and pick up 20 light pink beads and 2 bugles. Take the needle back through the delicas and through next loop below the bugle tube.

tip

Use cord thread for the tassel fringe so that it drapes nicely. Nymo thread is ideal for the brick stitch but will give a much stiffer effect if used for the tassel

6 Continue adding tassel strings around the bugle tube, alternating between dark and light beads and making the strings different lengths until there are sixteen strings in all. Sew the tassel to the bottom of the amulet purse.

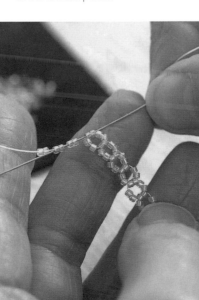

7 The strap is made using chain stitch (see page 23). Start by picking up 2 pink, 2 light pink, 2 pink and 2 light pink delicas and tie the beads into a circle. On the next and subsequent chains, pick up 2 light pink, 2 pink and 2 light pink delicas. Put the needle through the two pink beads at the top of the previous chain and through the first two light pink and pink beads just added. Work chain stitch until the strap is 60cm (23½in) long. Attach the strap securely on either side of the amulet purse.

beaded mules

Transform a pair of plain silk mules with these delightful paisley-pattern motifs. The motifs are worked in brick stitch using petite beads, which are the smallest seed beads, and have a pretty picot edging around the outside. These tiny beads make dainty motifs that can be stitched or glued on to the front of each shoe. The motifs are quite intricate and you will find it best to gain a little experience of stitching brick stitch (see page 21) before beginning as you will need to shape the design by introducing extra beads on the curves and adding beads to create the point.

beaded mules

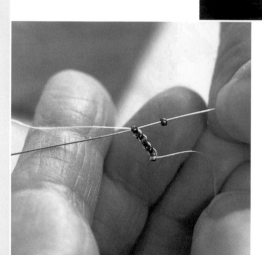

- pale pink Nymo thread
- size 13 beading needle
- 2g crystal petite beads
- 2g green rainbow petite beads
- 2g dark rainbow petite beads
- 4g crystal aqua petite beads
- 2g crystal pink petite beads
- 2g pale mauve petite beads
- scissors
- silk mules
- flat-nosed pliers

1 Thread the needle with a 1m (1yd) length of Nymo thread. Pick up a dark rainbow bead and put the needle back through the bead again. Pick up a second dark rainbow bead and put the needle back through the previous bead and then back through the one just added.

2 Add a further 4 dark rainbow beads and 3 aqua crystal beads. Take the needle through the last crystal bead again and then pick up 2 aqua crystal beads. Put the needle through the first loop and back through the second bead. Work brick stitch (see page 21) down the first side. Work 3 aqua crystal beads in the loop on the first rainbow bead and then work back up the second side in brick stitch.

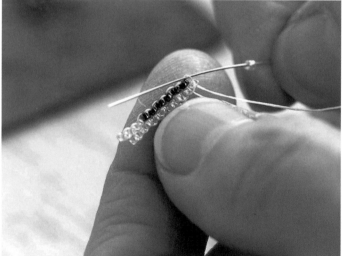

tip

It is much easier to make the paisley motifs using a magnifying lamp. The petite beads are very small and you will be able to pass the needle under loops more easily when they are magnified.

3 Bring the needle out at the top crystal bead and pick up two green rainbow beads. Work one row of brick stitch. To keep the motif flat, increase the number of beads around the bottom curve by working a second bead into a loop twice.

4 Work a second row of brick stitch. At the point end pick up a green rainbow bead and take the needle back through the bead on the opposite side to make a point. Add a row of dark rainbow beads.

try this
Make a matching brooch by stitching a beaded paisley motif and sticking it to fabric-covered card. Attach a brooch fastening to the back.

5 Beginning at the top bead on the motif work three rows of crystal aqua beads, tapering the beads to shape the motif. Add 6 crystal aqua beads to the point in the same method as step 1. Work a row of brick stitch back down to the motif and then feed the needle back through the beads to add a row of 5 more beads at the top and then another row of 3.

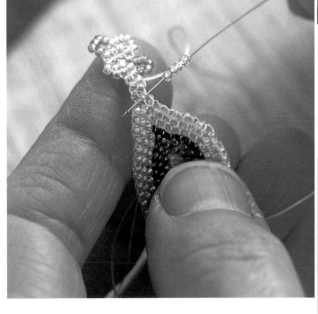

6 To make the picot edging, pick up 5 pale mauve beads. Miss a bead on the motif and take the needle down through the next. Bring it out at the next bead and pick up 5 crystal pink beads. Work round the motif alternating the colours.

7 Make three motifs for each mule, checking the arrangement of the motifs on the front of each mule. Secure a thread with a double backstitch under the first motif and stab stitch through the motif and the mule front to secure. Use a pair of flat-nosed pliers to pull the needle through. Finish off the thread under the motif and trim. Add the other two motifs to the mule in the same way. Repeat for the other mule.

zigzag necklace

Although it looks quite unassuming, this pretty necklace will hang beautifully around your neck, and because it is such a simple design you can easily change the colour of the beads to suit the colour of your outfit. The fringe has been designed to fit inside a 'V' neck but can be altered in length and shape to suit the neckline of any dress or top. The necklace is worked in square stitch, an ideal stitch for this design as it has a wonderful draping quality which allows the necklace to fall into the contours of your neck. For a more formal occasion, you could make a set of earrings to complement the necklace.

zigzag necklace

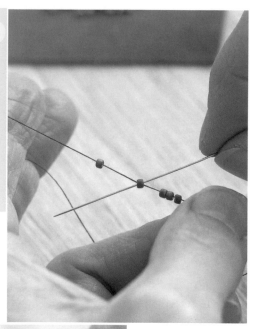

1 Thread your needle with a long length of red Nymo thread. To make the first block of 8 beads in square stitch (see page 20), string on 5 red seed beads. Take the needle back through the fourth bead and pull the thread tight so that the fifth bead is suspended below the fourth bead.

tip

To make the necklace as strong as possible, stabilize the blocks by taking the thread back though the last two rows of beads at every opportunity.

2 Put the needle back through the fifth bead and pick up another bead, the sixth. Put the needle back through the third bead and through the sixth bead again so that it is also suspended below the first row. Add the seventh and eighth beads in the same way.

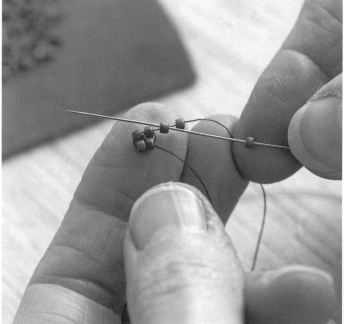

3 Take the needle back through the first four beads and down the second row to stabilize the block. Add another row of 4 beads and stabilize again.

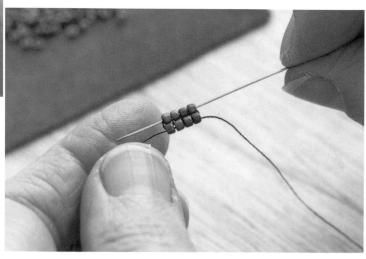

4 Pick up 5 beads. Put the needle back through the second last bead and through the last bead again. Work down the row of eight beads in square stitch.

5 Take the needle back through the last two rows twice bringing it out in the middle of the last row. Add 4 beads with square stitch and take the needle down through the first 4 beads on the previous row and back up the last row. Repeat steps 4 and 5 until there are 44 blocks of 16 beads.

6 To add the fringe, thread the needle with another long length of thread. With the ends of the zigzag facing up, take the needle through the first block of beads and out at the first 'V' of the zigzag.

7 Pick up a red bead, then a gold and another red. Take the needle back through the large bead and the first red bead. Feed the needle through the beads in the zigzag chain to the next V. Add a fringe strand of 3 beads at the next ten Vs.

8 On the next and subsequent Vs add on another red and gold bead each time until there are 12 gold beads in the centre of the necklace. Decrease the fringe strands two beads at a time to complete the other side of the necklace.

9 Attach a toggle fastening at each end. Secure the ends by threading back and forwards three times through the necklace and snip off the excess thread.

try this

Make a set of matching earrings by working seven rows of 8 beads in square stitch. Attach five fringe strands of 9 red beads and 8 gold beads to the block. Finish by stitching an earring hook to the top corner of the block.

bead-fringed cushion

This section features beaded fringes and tassels and shows how ordinary items can be transformed into something quite special. Cushions are one of the most creative pieces of soft furnishing and can be used in almost any room. Tucked in the corner of a chair, scattered on a sofa or arranged at the head of a bed, they add a splash of colour that can complement or lift a decorative scheme. Adding a beaded fringe will transform the plainest cushion and introduce texture and sparkle into a room. Choose fabrics with a slight sheen to complement the beads and add the fringe to a piece of grosgrain ribbon that matches the fabric.

bead-fringed cushion

you will need

- beading needle
- dark blue cord thread
- 41cm (16in) of 2cm (¾in) wide blue grosgrain ribbon
- 2g Caspian blue seed beads
- 2g frosted gunmetal seed beads
- 2g slate blue seed beads
- 2g frosted ice seed beads
- 6g blue iris seed beads
- 2g green iris seed beads
- 6g silver-lined clear size 8 seed beads
- scissors
- 0.5m (½yd) blue fabric
- 26 × 41cm (10 × 16in) cream fabric
- cream and blue sewing threads
- pins
- sewing machine
- 40cm (16in) square cushion pad

1 To make the beaded fringe, thread the beading needle with a length of dark blue cord thread and tie a knot in the end. Insert the needle through some threads on the reverse side of the ribbon 2cm (¾in) from the end and bring it out through one of the tiny loops on the edge.

2 Pick up one each of the following beads: Caspian blue, gunmetal, slate blue, frosted ice and green iris. Then pick up a blue iris and work back down the list in the opposite direction, picking up 11 beads in all. Pick up a clear size 8 bead and a blue iris. Ignoring the last bead threaded, take the needle back up through the beads and into the loop at the edge of the ribbon.

3 Oversew through the next three loops and then pick up the same order of beads as above. Pick up a further 4 blue iris beads and then take the needle through the clear crystal bead and back up the other beads.

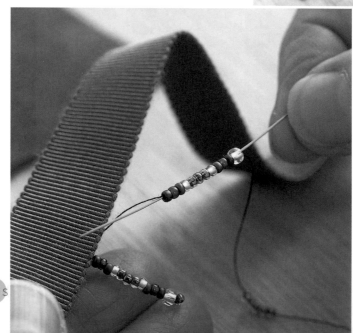

tip
If you can't find a grosgrain ribbon in a suitable colour, cover it with a satin or velvet ribbon that complements the fabrics.

4 These two strands are repeated along the ribbon to make the fringe. Stop on a longer strand about 2cm (¾in) from the end of the ribbon. Slip the thread through a few threads on the reverse side and take two small backstitches before trimming the excess thread.

5 To make the cushion, cut the following pieces from blue fabric: front panel 18 × 41cm (7 × 16in); back panels 24 × 41cm (9½ × 16in) and 34 × 41cm (13½ × 16in). Pin the cream fabric piece and the blue front panel right sides together along one long edge and machine stitch. Trim the seam and press towards the blue fabric. Pin the beaded ribbon along the edge of the blue fabric and, using a zipper foot, machine stitch along the edge of the ribbon next to the blue fabric.

try this
Make a rectangular cushion to match using a similar type of envelope opening in the back panel. Insert the beaded ribbon in the seam at each end of the cushion cover before stitching and turning through.

6 Press under a 6mm (¼in) turning and then a further 1cm (½in) hem along one long edge of each blue back panel and then machine stitch.

7 With right sides facing pin the small back panel along the top edge of the cushion. Lay the other panel on top with the hems overlapping and pin. Machine stitch all the way round the outside, double stitching where the hems overlap. Trim across the corners and turn the cover through. Press before inserting the cushion pad.

fringed lampshade

Although inspired by the ornate beaded lampshades found in Victorian boudoirs and lounges, this wonderful lampshade has a thoroughly modern look. Choose a bright contemporary colour for the lampshade and pick beads that complement the base of the lampshade too. This fringe uses shades of lilac and silver beads with a darker purple bauble at the end of each strand to add depth of colour and weight. The length of the fringe you make will depend on the height and width of your lampshade, and remember it doesn't have to be straight along the bottom - why not try a zigzag or curved fringe instead?

fringed lampshade

- 1.25cm (½in) wide seam tape, long enough to fit the shade
- beading needle
- cord beading thread
- 12g silver-lined crystal clear 3mm bugles
- 7g silver-lined crystal clear seed beads
- 7g lavender seed beads
- 7g violet/turquoise seed beads
- 7g silver-lined blueberry seed beads
- 7g violet rainbow seed beads
- 7g cobalt blue seed beads
- 20g deep blue rainbow seed beads
- scissors
- fabric glue
- glue brush
- 1.5cm (⅝in) satin ribbon, long enough to fit shade

1 Cut a piece of seam tape long enough to fit around the bottom edge of the lampshade, adding 4cm (1½in) seam allowance. Using cord thread, work a couple of backstitches into the tape at one end and bring the needle out at the edge of the tape 2cm (¾in) in.

2 To make the fringe, start by picking up a bugle then the beads in this order – lavender, violet/turquoise, silver-lined blueberry, violet rainbow, cobalt blue and deep blue rainbow. Miss the deep blue and work back down the list picking up 13 beads in all.

3 Repeat the sequence three times in all and then pick up 2 bugles. To make the bauble on the end, pick up 3 deep blue beads and put the needle back through the last bugle. Repeat five times in all.

4 Pick up a crystal clear seed bead and take the needle back through the bauble and the other beads in the strand. Secure the thread in the tape and then work running stitch along 6mm (¼in), ready to make the next strand. Repeat until the fringe is long enough to fit around the lampshade.

tip
You will need to use a size 13 beading needle and fine beading thread so that you can stitch through the bugle several times when making the bauble at the end of the fringe.

5 Lay the finished fringe on a flat surface. Brush a thin layer of fabric glue along the reverse side of the tape. Lift the tape carefully and stick along the bottom edge of the lampshade. You may need a friend to help at this stage. Trim the ends and slipstitch together.

6 To finish, cut a piece of satin ribbon to fit around the lampshade. Pin the ribbon in place, fold under the raw edges at one corner and slipstitch the edges together. Sew a few tiny stitches on both edges of the ribbon at each corner to secure.

try this
If you can't find a lampshade in the colour you require you can cover a lampshade with silk/viscose velvet backed with Lamitex. This is a matt sheet that can be cut to size and ironed on to the reverse side of the fabric. Fold the top and bottom edges of the fabric over the lampshade rings and stick on the inside.

devoré scarf

An elegant scarf is ideal for keeping the chill off your shoulders when wearing an evening gown. A net fringe adds colour and sparkle to a plain scarf and the weight of the beads helps to hold the scarf in place. Different effects can be achieved depending on how you shade the seed beads from dark to light between the pearls. I have given the order and colours of the beads I used but choosing your own colour scheme is half the fun. Devoré velvet is made from silk georgette with a viscose pile. The pattern on the scarf is created with etching fluid, which removes the unwanted viscose pile, leaving the plain silk georgette in some areas.

devoré scarf

you will need

- silk/viscose scarf
- masking tape
- pencil
- ruler
- cord thread
- beading needle
- 20g 4mm gold pearls
- 28g 4mm dark brown pearls
- 28g burnt orange seed beads
- 28g orange seed beads
- 28g apricot seed beads

1 Stick a length of masking tape across the width of the scarf and stick the ends to the work surface. Measure the width of the scarf and mark approximately every 2cm (¾in) along the tape.

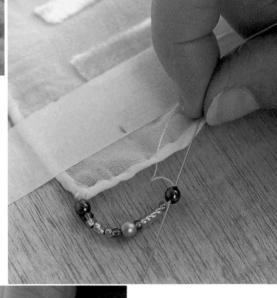

2 Beginning at one corner, attach a length of cord thread and pick up 1 dark brown pearl, 6 seed beads (1 burnt orange, 1 orange, 2 apricot, 1 orange and 1 burnt orange were used here), 1 gold pearl, 6 seed beads (as before) and 1 dark brown pearl. Take a tiny stitch into the scarf below the second mark then put the needle back through the dark brown pearl. Work across the scarf adding the same loop of beads between the marks. Sew in the end.

3 Secure a second thread with a couple of tiny stitches on the reverse side and bring it out through the first dark brown pearl. Pick up 8 seed beads (1 burnt orange, 2 orange, 2 apricot, 2 orange and 1 burnt orange were used here), then 1 brown pearl. Repeat three times. Add another string of beads down the other side.

4 Take a new length of thread up through the second dark brown bead at one side. Pick up 6 seed beads (order as in step 2) and take the needle through the gold pearl. Pick up another 6 seed beads (as before) and 1 dark brown pearl. Continue like this across the width.

try this

If you can't find a scarf in the right colour, simply buy a white silk/viscose scarf and dye it to match the beads. See suppliers list on page 111 for scarf stockists.

5 At the other end take the needle down through the dark brown pearl at the end. Work back across, feeding the needle through the dark brown heads. Continue adding rows of bead netting until you reach the last dark brown bead at each side.

tip

When you need a new thread, join the ends together with a reef knot (see page 15) and sew the ends back through several beads before trimming close to the netting.

6 Pick up 21 seed beads (order as in step 3 until there are 21 beads), 1 dark brown pearl and 1 burnt orange seed bead. Take the needle back through the dark brown pearl, the seed beads and the next dark brown pearl. Pick up 6 seed beads (as in step 2), feed the needle through the gold pearl at the bottom of the netting and pick up another 6 seed beads (as before) and 1 brown pearl. Repeat until the fringe and last row of netting is complete. Sew in thread ends securely.

devoré scarf 71

tasselled key-rings

It will be difficult to misplace your keys when they are attached to wonderful tasselled key-rings that are not only practical but decorative too. The tassels can be made in a single colour to match your décor or in a combination of mixed colours for a different effect. Attach a beaded tassel to your key with some beautiful sheer ribbon for an elegant, artistic touch. Beaded tassels can also be attached to the corners of large square cushions and used to finish the flat end of bolsters.

tasselled key-rings

you will need

- quilting thread to match beads
- beading needle
- 22mm (⅞in) wooden bead
- 10g lime seed beads (or fuchsia)
- 12g lime 6mm (¼in) bugles (or fuchsia)
- scissors

1 Thread a length of quilting thread on to the beading needle and feed it through the centre of the wooden bead and tie with a surgeon's knot (see page 15). Pick up approximately 17 seed beads and put the needle back through the centre of the wooden bead. Hold your finger and thumb over the holes to stop the beads going in and then pull the thread tight.

tip

The tassel is much more tactile if you use quilting thread or another strong corded thread to make the strings. Nymo thread is rather stiff and will give a firmer finish to the tassel.

2 Continue adding 17 beads at a time until the bead strands touch near the holes with gaps in the middle – about 12 altogether. Now pick up 13 beads each time and fill every second gap around the wooden bead. Fill the remaining gaps with groups of 9 beads. Tie the thread ends together with a surgeon's knot and trim the ends.

3 To make the tassel loop, pick up 25 beads on a length of quilting thread. Feed the needle back through the beads to form a circle and then take it back through again for extra strength. Put both ends into the needle and take them through the wooden bead.

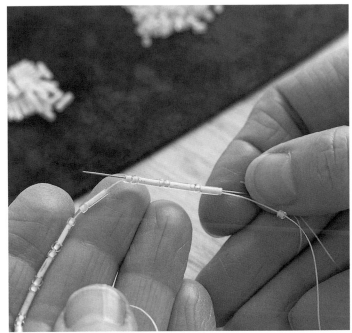

4 Thread a 2m (2¼yd) length of quilting thread on to the needle. Pick up 2 seed beads and a bugle bead. Repeat until there are 8 bugle beads on the thread. Pick up another seed bead. Leaving the last seed bead take the needle back through the other beads. Ease the bead string down the thread until there is a 10cm (4in) tail.

try this

Make a spiral staircase loop (see spiral bracelet, page 42) long enough to fit around a napkin and attach the tassel to make a stunning napkin ring.

5 Keep adding further strings of beads and bugles until there are ten strings altogether. Tie the thread ends together and split the tassel string bundle in two. Loop the threads sticking out from the bottom of the wooden bead around the tassel strings and tie off using a surgeon's knot. Trim the thread ends.

6 Thread another 2m (2¼yd) length of thread and secure the end to the base of the wooden bead close to the tassel strings. Thread on the seed beads and bugles to make a tassel string as in steps 4 and 5. Take the needle under one of the adjacent threads on the wooden bead and make another tassel string. Keep working around the wooden bead adding tassel strings until there are forty in all. Sew in the end and trim neatly to finish.

beaded notebook

Exquisite beadwork embroidery transforms a simple notebook or address book into something really special. By choosing beads that tone in with the fabric, the overall effect is subtle with a mix of couched bugles and seed beads creating a simple, textured surface. This beaded cover is not only beautiful but is practical too, as it is designed to be slipped off and fitted on to another notebook when required. Choose a luxury fabric such as silk dupion that will show the beads off at their best, and back the silk fabric with thin quilting wadding (batting) to give it an opulent feel.

beaded notebook

you will need

- two pieces 40 x 26cm (16 x 10in) of silk dupion
- 40 x 26cm (16 x 10in) thin wadding (batting)
- A6 notebook
- vanishing embroidery marker
- ruler
- tapestry needle
- rotary frame
- beading needle
- 10g pale coral seed beads
- 10g dark coral seed beads
- 10g pink pearl seed beads
- 18g small coral bugle beads
- scissors
- coral sewing thread
- sewing needle
- tacking (basting) thread
- sewing machine

1 Lay one piece of silk dupion on top of the wadding (batting) and fold in half crossways to mark the centre line. Position the notebook just right of the centre line. Mark the corners with a vanishing embroidery marker.

tip

Allow for the thickness of the notebook cover when marking and stitching. It is better that the cover is slightly too big than too tight a fit, so check your measurements carefully before stitching by machine.

2 Score between the first two dots with a tapestry needle and ruler and tack (baste) along the line. Repeat on all sides. Fit the silk and wadding (batting) into a rotary frame.

3 Thread the beading needle with coral thread and secure on the back with two small backstitches. Bring it out on the right side in the top corner of the tacked (basted) outline. Pick up a pale coral seed bead and then a bugle. Continue adding beads until there are 13 bugles and 12 seed beads. Insert the beading needle into the fabric below the tacked (basted) line at top left and wrap the thread around the beading needle several times to tension it.

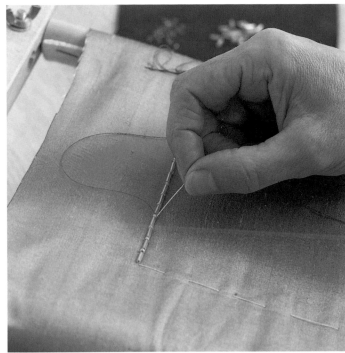

4 Thread a sewing needle with another length of coral thread. Secure it to the wadding (batting) and bring it out below the first seed bead. Couch between each bead, working along the line of beads (see couching, page 25). Couch the same order of beads along the bottom tacked (basted) line. Now couch a row of 17 bugles and 18 seed beads between the two beaded lines along the left-hand side tacking (basting) thread. Repeat the same order for a line of couched beads on the right side.

5 Now bead the area inside the bead border from the bottom up, as follows. For the first row, pick up a pale coral, a pink pearl, a pale coral and a pink pearl bead, repeating this order until there are approximately 80 beads strung. Couch the beads as before. For the second row repeat the order but on every alternate bugle row use dark coral beads instead of pale coral beads. Fill the area inside the bead border alternating these two rows. Once all the beading is complete, take the fabric and wadding (batting) off the frame and press the fabric lightly.

6 To make up the notebook cover, lay the fabric face down on the plain piece of silk and mark the outline of the open notebook on the wadding (batting) using a fabric marker. Trim along the lines. Extend the lines out 5cm (2in) on each side of the book for the flaps. Score the fabric to mark the stitching lines at each end and tack (baste) the two pieces of silk together along the top and bottom of the wadding and around the flaps.

7 Fit a sewing machine with a zipper foot so that you can stitch close to the beads. Stitch just outside the tacked (basted) line all round, leaving a gap for turning at one end. Trim across the corners. Trim the seam allowances to 6mm (¼in).

8 Turn the beaded cover through. Slipstitch the gap and press the cover if necessary. Fold the front flap back 5cm (2in) and slipstitch it to the front cover with tiny stitches.

9 Tuck the book into the first flap and fold the back flap inside. Check that it closes before slipstitching the back flap in position.

try this

Do you love the idea of a beaded notebook cover but are rather short of time? Try stitching a grid of machine stitching inside the tacked (basted) outline of the notebook and then fill every other square with a little circle of beads.

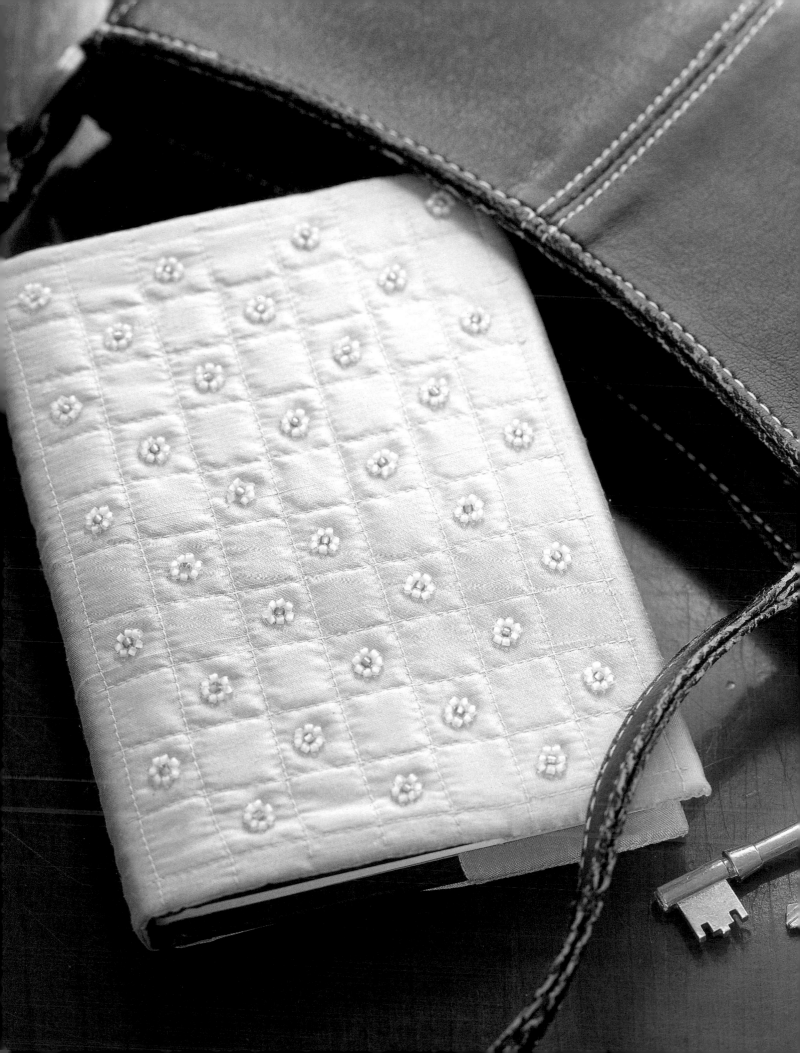

sequined decorations

These delightful padded shapes prove that decorations are not just for Christmas but for any special occasion. The sequins and beads are sewn on in loops to create an interesting three-dimensional surface which catches the light, so hang them in the corner of a room or from a pergola in a summer garden where they will sparkle as they turn. Choose beads and sequins that match the colour of the fabric or dye the fabric to match the beads – diluting the dye to create delicate pastel shades.

sequined decorations

1 The instructions are for the heart decoration – use the picture on page 83 as a guide for making the other shapes. Begin by enlarging the heart template on page 109 by 200%, and cut out the shape. Place two pieces of velvet right sides together and pin a template to one side. Machine stitch around the edge of the template leaving a gap on one side for turning.

2 Trim the seam allowance to 6mm (¼in) and trim across the corners to reduce the bulk. Snip into the point at the top of the heart. Notch the outer curves for ease of turning. Turn the shape through to the right side, easing out the corners, and stuff with polyester stuffing. Slipstitch the gap.

tip

When making the star decoration, trim across the points of the star and then trim close to the stitching down both sides of each point before turning through. Carefully ease the points out with a knitting needle or bodkin.

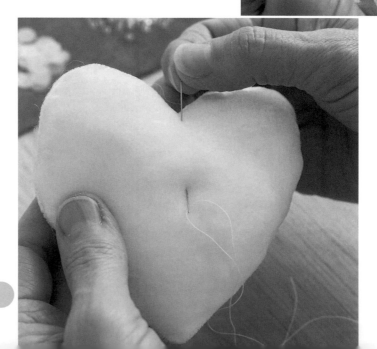

3 Thread the beading needle with sewing thread and tie an overhand knot (see page 15) at the end. Take a stitch into the centre of the decoration and tug to bury the knot in the stuffing.

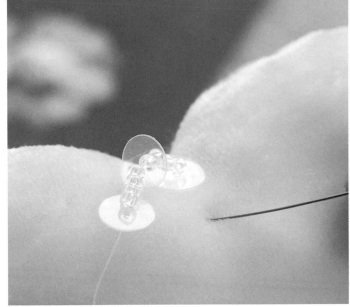

4 Using the colours of your choice, pick up 1 sequin, 4 seed beads, 1 sequin, 4 seed beads and then a final sequin. Put the needle into the decoration so that the last sequin will sit next to the first.

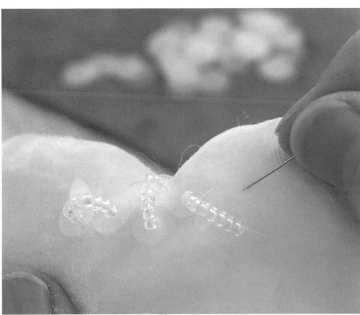

5 Bring the needle back out between the two sequins and slightly in front. Repeat step 4 so that this group of beads lies perpendicular to the first group. Continue adding groups of beads and sequins in a grid-like pattern until the front of the decoration is covered.

6 To hang, attach a double sewing thread at the top of the decoration. Pick up enough seed beads to make a cord about 30cm (12in) long. Carefully tie a small loop at the top and feed the end of the thread back through the beads.

try this

If you want to hang the decorations on a Christmas tree, make a loop by picking up 45 seed beads. Take the needle back into the top of the decoration, take two tiny backstitches and then a large stitch through the decoration and trim off the end of the thread.

7 On the heart and diamond decorations, attach a thread to the bottom of the decoration. Pick up 4 seed beads and 1 sequin. Repeat until there are 7 sequins. Pick up a further 4 seed beads. Miss the last seed bead and take the needle back through the other beads and sequins. Secure the thread to finish.

pot-pourri sachets

These little beaded cushions will fill your bedroom with the wonderful scent of roses all year round. The scent can be refreshed from time to time with a few drops of rose oil. Use the sachets individually to tuck in a drawer or tie the three together with a pretty ribbon to decorate the dressing table. Choose delicate pastel shades of silk organza to make the cushions to allow the rose pot-pourri to show through the sheer fabric. An added layer of tulle over the silk organza gives a slightly antique appearance.

pot-pourri sachets

- pencil and fine black marker
- pale green silk organza
- pale cream silk organza
- pale pink silk organza
- pale pink tulle
- scissors
- vanishing embroidery marker
- tacking (basting) thread
- sewing needle
- beading needle
- 18cm (7in) embroidery hoop
- 5g mid green seed beads
- 5g light green seed beads
- 5g crystal green seed beads
- 5g pink seed beads
- 5g pale pink seed beads
- sewing thread
- sewing machine
- rose pot-pourri
- 1m (1yd) of 15mm (⅝in) pale green sheer organza ribbon

tip

Stitch all the outline beads at one sitting as the marked design will vanish in a few hours.

1 Trace the design on page 109 and outline with a black marker. Cut a 25cm (10in) square in pale green silk organza and one in pale pink tulle. Position the template under the organza with the tulle on top and trace the design with a vanishing embroidery marker.

2 Tack (baste) around the square border and then fit the two fabrics into an embroidery hoop. Thread both needles with lengths of sewing thread and secure each length inside one of the petal shapes with two tiny backstitches.

3 With the beading needle, pick up one each of the green beads and repeat until there are sufficient to fit along the first curved line of the motif. Couch the beads down with the other needle and thread (see couching, page 25). Work all four sides in the same way.

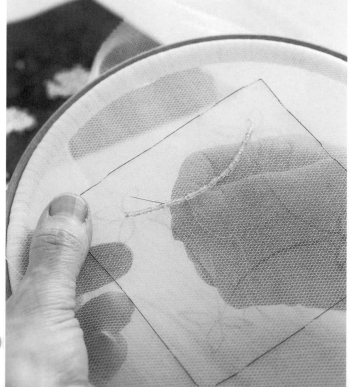

4 Pick up 11 pink beads and couch down one side of the middle petal. Couch 10 pink beads down the other side of the petal. On the side petals put the needle through the first two beads of the middle petal and then pick up only 9 beads. Couch 10 beads down the remaining sides.

try this

Using the same bead design, you could make a large cushion with the design embroidered in the centre. Tuck a rose pot-pourri sachet in the middle of the stuffing before closing the gap.

5 Fill the petals with pale pink seed beads stitched on individually from the reverse side. Now take the embroidery out of the hoop and press the fabric carefully.

6 Cut three 15cm (6in) squares of pale green organza and steam press together. Place these squares on top of the bead embroidery right sides together and pin. Machine stitch just inside the tacked (basted) line leaving a gap on one side.

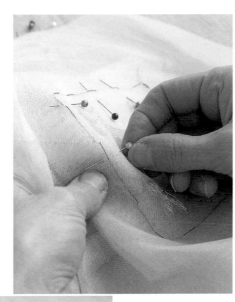

7 Trim the seam allowance to 6mm (¼in) and trim across corners. Turn through and ease out corners.

8 Fill the sachet with rose pot-pourri and slipstitch the gap. Make a pale pink and cream sachet in the same way but without any bead embroidery. Pile the sachets together and tie in a bundle with some sheer organza ribbon.

bead-embellished bag

Whether you're off to the shops or going out for the day, this stylish rucksack-type bag is ideal for all your bits and bobs. It is the perfect style of bag for a day in town as your hands are free to pick things up and to open doors. It is very easy to make, as it is really just a simple drawstring bag so why not make another for a day at the beach or to suit your usual colour scheme? For a beach bag, choose a bright, sunny fabric with colourful beads or use fabric and beads that complement your favourite outfit.

bead-embellished bag

you will need

- 3 × 38cm (5 × 15in) antique white linen
- 3 × 38cm (5 × 15in) iron-on interfacing
- tacking (basting) thread
- sewing needle
- vanishing embroidery marker
- beading needle
- white quilting thread
- 12g purple/olive matt seed beads
- 12g brown satin matt seed beads
- 12g stone matt seed beads
- 12g medium grey matt seed beads
- 12g of 3mm (⅛in) purple/olive bugle beads
- two pieces 56 × 38cm (22 × 15in) raw linen
- sewing thread
- scissors
- pins
- sewing machine
- two 2m (2¼yd) lengths of white cord
- two large eyelets and eyelet tool

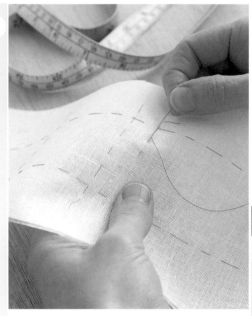

1 Iron the interfacing on to the reverse side of the antique white linen. Tack (baste) two lines 5cm (2in) apart down the centre of the linen strip. Now tack (baste) lines across, to make five 5cm (2in) squares, 1.5cm (⅝in) apart along the strip (see diagram on page 109).

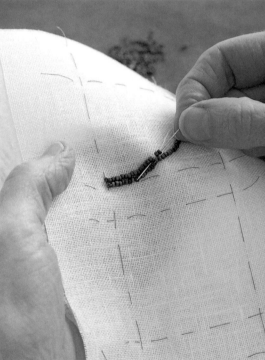

2 Using the vanishing marker, draw a curve on the right-hand square. Using quilting thread stitch a row of purple/olive beads with backstitch along the line. Continue filling in the area below the curve with beads and then fill in the last corner. Mark the next square into nine equal squares. Stitch brown satin beads in each little square, alternating the rows from horizontal to vertical.

3 On the middle square, divide the square into four equal vertical strips and work zigzag rows of stone matt beads to cover the area. In the next square begin stitching bugles around the outside edge and then work into the centre, completing a triangle each time. On the left-hand square use medium grey matt beads, beginning in the centre and spiralling out to make a circle. Fill in the corners to complete the square.

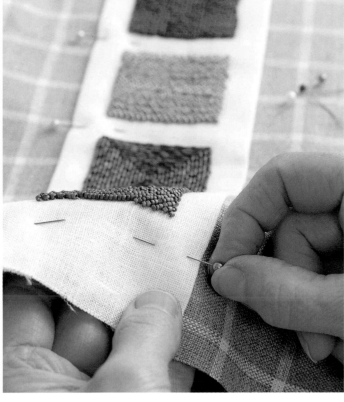

4 To make up the bag, remove the tacking (basting) thread. Turn under 2cm (¾in) down the long edges of the strip and pin it across one piece of the raw linen 10cm (4in) from the bottom. Machine stitch in place close to the edge.

5 Pin the two pieces of linen right sides together and machine stitch the side seams and along the bottom. Leaving 8cm (3in) clear at the top of each side seam, zigzag the seams and trim. Turn the bag through to the right side and press. Stitch diagonally across both bottom corners 4cm (1½in) from the point (the eyelets will be positioned here later).

try this

If you are short of time, stitch the beads in a pattern so that they are less solidly packed and make the bag up as shown in the steps.

6 To make a channel around the top edge, turn down 2cm (¾in) and then a further 3cm (1¼in) and pin. Machine stitch close to the hem edge and again along the top edge. Snip into the side seams between the casing lines. Thread the lengths of white cord through the casing, one from each side.

tip

Dip the white cotton cord in a very weak tea solution. This will darken it slightly so that it is not so stark and matches the antique linen.

7 Following the manufacturer's instructions fit an eyelet into each bottom corner of the bag. Feed the pairs of white cords through the eyelets and tie the ends in an overhand knot (see page 15) to complete.

coiled coasters

Using beads with wire is the theme for this section, so start by giving your dining table extra style with these eye-catching beaded coasters. These bright pink beads have a fresh summery feel to them but you could use any colour to co-ordinate with your existing tableware. As the beads are very small and packed closely together, they form a smooth surface on which to place your glass. Presented in a pretty, shimmering mesh bag, a set of six of these bead coasters would form a lovely gift. Or why not make a larger version of the coaster design as a pretty addition to any dressing table.

coiled coasters

1 Cut a 2.5m (2¾yd) length of wire and pick up a seed bead. Fold the first 1cm (⅜in) of the wire over the bead and twist to secure. Pour a small quantity of beads into your left hand (right hand if you are left-handed). Holding the other end of the wire, pick up about 10 beads at a time and let them drop down the wire.

tip

You can buy beads already strung – just loop the wire over the thread at one end and feed the beads on to the wire.

2 Keep picking up beads and letting them drop down the wire until the handful is finished. Continue pouring beads into the palm of your hand and feeding them on to the wire until there is a 2m (2¼yd) length.

3 Make a loop on the end of the wire to prevent the beads falling off. Now cut five 30cm (12in) lengths of wire and fold each in half. Tuck one of the pieces of wire over the first bead and cross over the ends to secure it.

4 Add the other four pieces of wire in the same way, leaving a bead between each wire. These are the spoke wires. Now begin to coil the beaded wire. At each spoke wire cross the wires over between two beads.

5 Keep coiling the beaded wire and crossing over the spoke wires. The spokes should be evenly spaced at an angle of about 72 degrees. Continue until the coaster is about 7.5cm (3in) in diameter.

try this

Make an organza bag in which to keep the coasters. Pin two 30 x 12cm (12 x 4¾in) pieces of organza together and machine stitch around the edge leaving a gap. Trim the seams and cut across corners then turn through and press. Fold into three and oversew the side seams. Draw a swirl on the front flap and sew beads along the line.

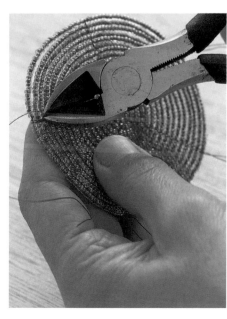

6 Fold the ends of the spokes back over the outside row of beads and trim the wire close to the beads. Remove any beads that remain on the wire beyond the last spoke. Fold the wire back and weave it into the coaster for a row or two. Snip the end close to the coaster to finish.

sparkling candlesticks

These days meal times are becoming increasingly casual, with ready-made meals and TV dinners the norm, but there are still some meals that merit a little extra effort. These two elegant candlesticks decorated with spirals of beaded wire will add a touch of glamour to the simplest table setting to make it fit for any special occasion. Choose a fresh colour scheme such as lilac and white to match your décor, or one that reflects the occasion. White and gold would look stunning for a christening or wedding breakfast whereas deep red and green are ideal at Christmas time.

sparkling candlesticks

you will need

- 1.25m (48in) of 1mm (19swg) silver-plated wire
- 10m (5½yd) of 0.4mm (27swg) silver-plated wire
- round-nosed pliers
- wire cutters
- safety glasses
- 5g frosted pale lilac seed beads
- 5g matt lilac seed beads
- 5g heather seed beads
- 5g lilac iris seed beads
- 10 white opal hearts
- 10 amethyst hearts
- 10 white opal flowers
- 10 amethyst flowers
- 20 amethyst pony beads
- two 18cm (7in) tall glass pillar candlesticks

try this

Why not create a set of matching napkin rings by making 25cm (10in) lengths of beaded wire to coil around a napkin?

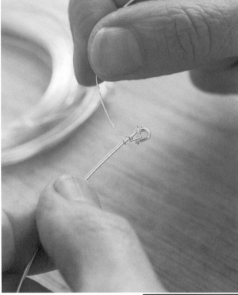

1 Cut a 60cm (24in) length of 1mm wire and bend over one end using round-nosed pliers. Cut a 1.5m (1¾yd) length of 0.4mm wire and attach one end to the bent end of the wire. Wrap the thin wire down the core wire a couple of times.

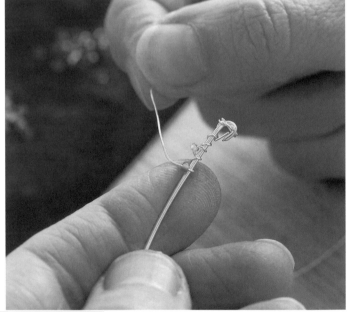

2 Pick up a pale lilac and a matt lilac seed bead and let them drop down to the work. Wrap the thin wire around the core wire several times, trapping both seed beads as you go. Wrap 2 seed beads on to the core wire between each of the following.

3 Pick up 7 heather seed beads and let them drop down to the work. Make a loop with the thin wire. Hold the seed beads at the top of the loop and twist to form a 6mm (¼in) stem.

4 Pick up a white opal heart. Make a loop as before and twist the heart to form a stem. Make a cluster with 7 lilac iris seed beads. Add a pony bead in the same way as the heart followed by a cluster of 7 heather beads.

tip

Wear safety glasses while cutting and wrapping the wire to protect your eyes and prevent an accident.

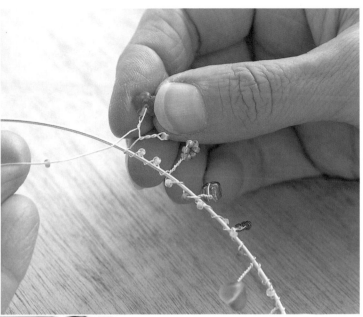

5 Pick up a pale lilac seed bead, a flower and another pale lilac seed bead. Fold the wire back over the first seed bead leaving a 1cm (½in) stem. Twist the stem halfway down. Hold the flower bead 7mm (⅜in) away and twist to form a short stem.

6 Twist the stem for the seed bead on the other side and then twist all the beads together to complete the stem down to the core wire. Repeat this sequence five times in all, alternating the colours of the hearts and flowers.

7 To finish, bend the end of the core wire over and wrap the thin wire around to secure, trimming the excess wire. Wrap the beaded wire around the stem of the candlestick and secure by hooking each end of the wire over where it meets the beaded wire.

flower gift bags

Pretty gift bags are the ideal way to wrap an awkwardly shaped present and can make even the smallest gift seem quite special and substantial. One or two lipsticks or bottles of nail polish make a wonderful gift for a teenager if presented in one of these delightful little bags and you can easily make a simple card to match. Enlarge the diagram on page 108 and make your own bag using crisp handmade paper, or decorate a ready-made bag. Change the colour to suit the occasion – off-white paper and gold beads would be ideal for a wedding gift.

flower gift bags

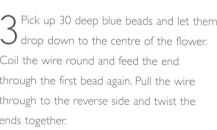

1 To make the wire flowers, start by cutting a 45cm (18in) length of wire and bend one end over 5cm (2in). Pick up 15 pale blue seed beads on the long end and let them drop down to the bend.

tip

Choose a crisp paper that will hold a crease well and which is thick enough to support the weight of the bead flowers and handles.

2 Bend the wire over at the other end of the beads. Pick up another 15 pale blue beads. Hold the beads between your finger and thumb and twist round once or twice. Make 5 petals in all, leaving the long end protruding from the centre.

3 Pick up 30 deep blue beads and let them drop down to the centre of the flower. Coil the wire round and feed the end through the first bead again. Pull the wire through to the reverse side and twist the ends together.

4 Cut six 20cm (8in) lengths of wire. Fill 18cm (7in) of each wire with beads, making 2 deep pink strands, 2 mid blue and 2 baby blue. Now plait one of each colour together to make the handles using masking tape to hold one end.

try this

Why not make a simple greetings card to match the gift bags? Fold a piece of white card in two. Tear a square of handmade paper and punch a hole in the centre and feed the wire ends of the flower through. Secure the wires with tape and stick to the front of the card.

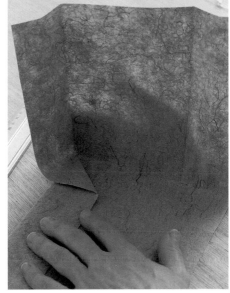

5 To make the paper bag, use the diagram on page 108, transferring the lines of the design on to the silk paper. Pre-crease the paper along the lines as indicated – dotted lines are 'mountain' folds and other dashed lines are 'valley' folds. Fold the side sections in one at a time. Fold the edge along the centre diagonal and then fold the other edge up. Secure at the top with a small piece of double-sided tape.

6 Turn under the top edge. Snip two notches on each side of the bag and tuck the handles in. Open out the bag flap, spread out the wire ends of the handles and stick a piece of double-sided tape across the wire ends. Fold the flap back down to secure.

7 Using a tapestry needle, punch a hole for each of the flowers in the front of the bag. Trim the flower wires and feed the ends through a hole. Open out the wire on the inside and use a sticky-backed label on the inside to secure each flower.

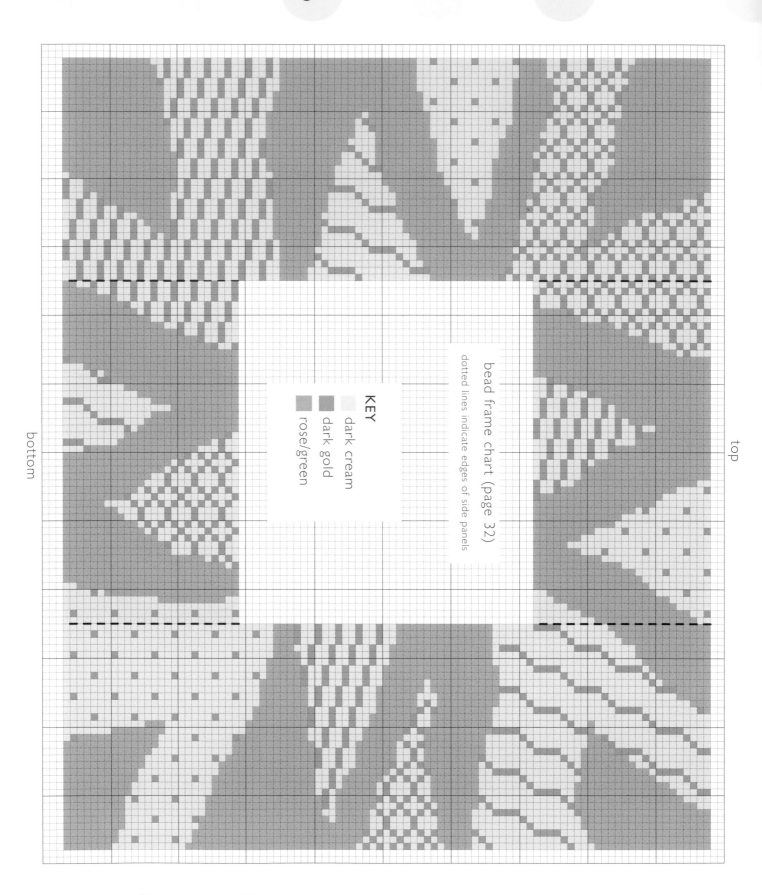

bottom

top

KEY

dark cream

dark gold

rose/green

bead frame chart (page 32)

dotted lines indicate edges of side panels

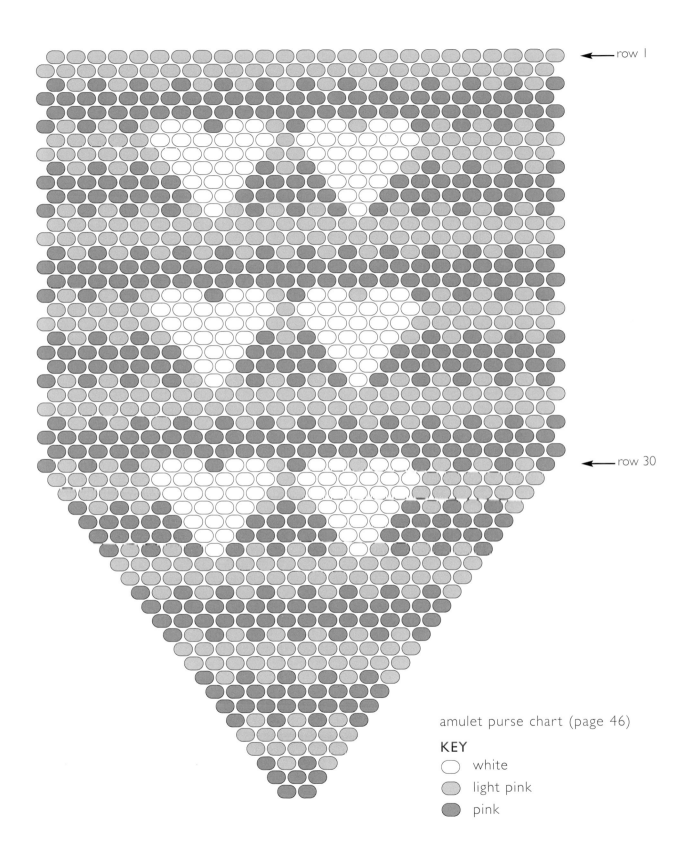

← row 1

← row 30

amulet purse chart (page 46)

KEY

◯ white

◯ light pink

● pink

trinket box chart (page 36)   card chart (page 36)

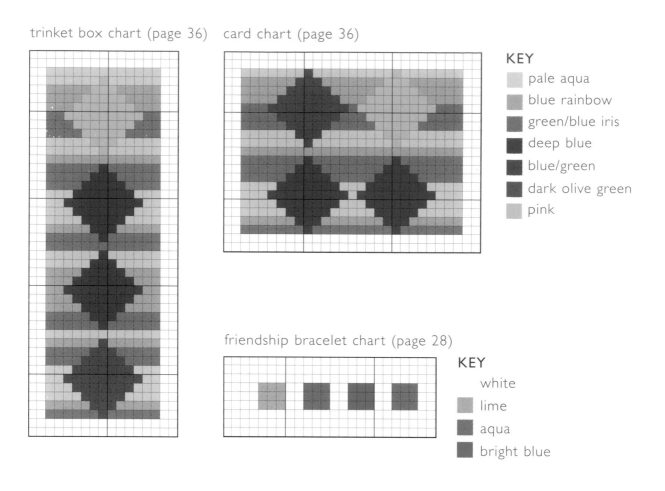

KEY
- pale aqua
- blue rainbow
- green/blue iris
- deep blue
- blue/green
- dark olive green
- pink

friendship bracelet chart (page 28)

KEY
- white
- lime
- aqua
- bright blue

flower gift bag diagram, page 102

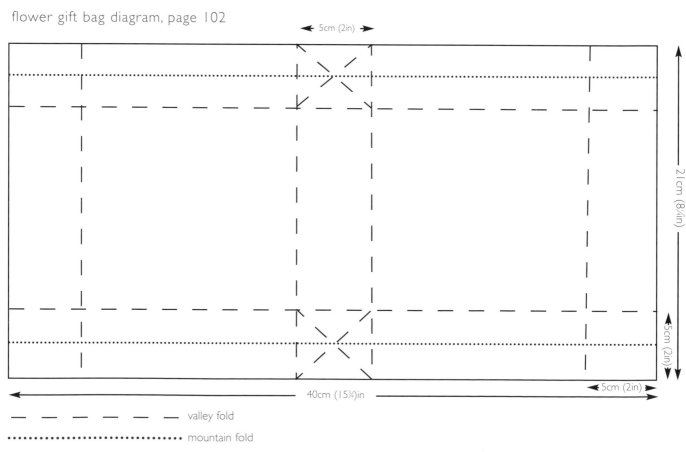

5cm (2in)

21cm (8¼in)

5cm (2in)

5cm (2in)

40cm (15¾in)

– – – – – – – – valley fold

•••••••••••••••• mountain fold

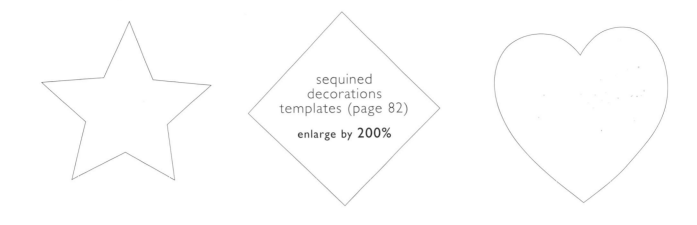

sequined
decorations
templates (page 82)

enlarge by **200%**

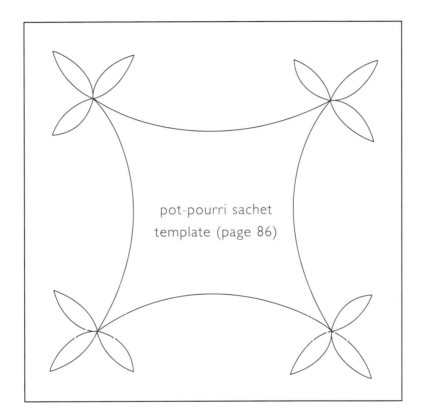

pot-pourri sachet
template (page 86)

bead-embellished bag
diagram (page 90)

enlarge by **200%**

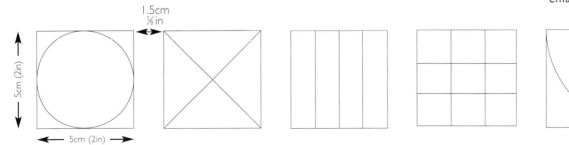

1.5cm
⅝in

5cm (2in)

5cm (2in)

bead project details

This list contains details of the various beads used in the projects, giving their specific colours and codes. However, the list is not exhaustive, and the availability of beads can change. The list of suppliers on the facing page will assist you in sourcing a vast variety of beads and accessories for your projects.

friendship bracelet (page 28)
Beadbox – delicas:
White lustre D201, limeaid D237, aqua D79, medium blue iris D76.

bead frame (page 32)
Beadbox – delicas:
Matt dark gold metallic D334, OP medium flesh lustre D204, matt rose/green metallic D380.

trinket box (page 36)
Beadesign – size 11 seed beads:
Pale aqua T0170D, rainbow multi M0283, blue M0279, pink T0038, blue/blue M0386, peacock green M0147, forest green/deep blue T0384.

spiral bracelets (page 42)
London Bead Company – hex and size 11 and 8 seed beads:
Size 8 aqua green 335, hex bright green 259, hex green 452; Size 11 mint green 336, grass green 547.

amulet purse (page 46)
Beadesign – delicas and 3mm bugles:
Bugles – SL crystal clear TB10021, lined light pink DBV 0082, pink DBV0106.
Beadbox – delicas white lustre D201.

beaded mules (page 50)
Mill Hill Beads – petite beads:
Crystal 40161, tapestry teal 42029, rainbow 40374, crystal aqua 42017, crystal pink 42018, heather mauve 42024.

zigzag necklace (page 54)
Beadbox – size 11 and 8 seed beads:
SL ruby multi matt 21202, SL gold matt 28352.

bead-fringed cushion (page 60)
Mill Hill Beads – size 11 seed beads:
Caspian blue 03027, frosted gunmetal 62021, slate blue 03010, frosted ice 62010, blue iris 03047, shimmering sea 02087, mercury 00283.
London Bead Company – size 8 seed beads:
SL clear size 8 seed beads 034.

fringed lampshade (page 64)
Beadesign – size 11 seed beads and 3mm bugles:
Seed beads – SL crystal clear T0021, CL lavender M0269, CL violet/turquoise T0937, SL blueberry M0029, rainbow violet T0327, cobalt blue T0116, rainbow deep blue T0408;
Bugles – SL crystal clear TB10021.

devoré scarf (page 68)
Gütermann – 4mm glass pearls and 9mm seed beads:
Pearls – dark brown 3350, gold 2885;
Seed beads – apricot 1345, orange 1850, burnt orange 1970.

tasselled key-rings (page 72)
London Bead Company – size 11 seed beads and 6mm bugles:
Lime 239, fuchsia 255.

beaded notebook (page 76)
Mill Hill Beads – size 11 seed beads and 6mm bugles:
Seed beads – frosted pink coral 62036, cherry sorbet 03057, tea rose 02004;
Bugles – peach crème 72003.

sequined decorations (page 82)
Gütermann – 9mm seed beads and 8mm flat sequins:
Seed beads – crystal 1030, aqua 7500, blue 6510;
Sequins – crystal 1030, aqua 7165, blue 6510.

pot-pourri sachets (page 86)
Beadesign – size 11 seed beads:
Adventurine green T0156, light French green M0143A, crystal green M0268A, pink M0168, pale pink T0011.

bead-embellished bag (page 90)
Beadesign – size 11 seed beads and 3mm bugles:
Seed beads – purple olive T0614, brown satin T0702, stone T0566, medium grey T0613;
Bugles – purple olive TB10614.

coiled coasters (page 94)
London Bead Company – size 11 seed beads:
Deep bright pink rainbow 309.

sparkling candlesticks (page 98)
Mill Hill Beads – size 11 seed beads, pebble beads and glass treasures:
Seed beads – frosted heather mauve 62024, matt lilac 02081, heather 02025, shimmering lilac 02084;
Pebble beads – amethyst 05202;
Glass treasures – hearts: opal 12090, amethyst 12091, flowers: opal 12297, amethyst 12295.

flower gift bags (page 102)
Beadesign – size 11 seed beads:
Baby pink T0145, blossom pink T0906, baby blue T0143, mid-blue T0917.

suppliers

UK Suppliers

ARTY'S
*For nearest stockist of silk/viscose velvet,
devoré scarves, dyes, lamitex (for backing
lampshades)*
Sinotex UK Ltd
Unit D, The Courtyard Business Centre
Lonesome Lane, Reigate
Surrey RH2 7QT
tel: 01737 245450
fax: 01737 247447
email: ww@artys.co.uk
www.artys.com

Beadbox
tel: (480) 967 4080
fax: (480) 967 8555
www.beadbox.com

Homecrafts direct
For bead looms
tel: 0116 269 7733
fax: 0116 269 7722
www.homecrafts.co.uk

Gütermann Beads
For nearest stockist:
Perivale-Gütermann Ltd
Bullsbrook Road, Hayes
Middlesex UB4 0JR
tel: 0208 589 1600
fax: 0208 589 1644
UK email: perivale@guetermann.com
Europe email: mail@guetermann.com

London Bead Company
339 Kentish Town Road
Kentish Town
London NW5 2TJ
tel: 0207 267 9403
fax: 0207 284 2062
www.londonbeadco.co.uk

Mill Hill Beads
Framecraft Miniatures Ltd
Lichfield Road, Brownhills
Walsall
West Midlands WS8 6LH
tel/fax: 01543 313 076

The Scientific Wire Company
18 Raven Road
London E18 1HW
tel: 0208 505 0002
fax: 0208 559 1114
www.wires.co.uk

The Spellbound Bead Company
45 Tamworth Street
Lichfield
Staffordshire WS13 6JW
tel: 01543 417650
www.spellboundbead.co.uk

US Suppliers

ARTY'S
*For nearest stockist of silk/viscose velvet,
devoré scarves, dyes*
Janlynn
tel: 1-800-445-5565
fax: 1-800-526-5966
email: janlynnsrv@aol.com

Beadbox
1290 N. Scottsdale Road
Tempe, Arizona 85281-1703
tel: 1-800-232-3269
fax: 1-800-242-3237
www.beadbox.com

Gütermann of America Inc
8227 Arrowridge Blvd
Post office box 7387
Charlotte, NC 28241-7387
tel: (704) 525-7068
fax: (704) 525-7071
email: info@gutermann-us.com

Mill Hill Beads
For nearest stockist:
Gay Bowles Sales Inc
PO Box 1060, Janesville
WI 53547-1060
tel: (608) 754-9466
fax: (608) 754-0665
www.millhill.com

acknowledgments

I would like to thank the following companies for so generously supplying beads for this book: Beadbox, Beadesign, Framecraft Miniatures (UK) Ltd, Gay Bowles Sales Inc. and Perivale-Gütermann. I would also like to thank ARTY's for the supply of silk/viscose velvet, scarf and fibre reactive dyes for the devoré scarf, fringed lampshade and bead decorations, and Homecrafts direct for the bead loom.

Thanks to the editorial team who gave me lots of support and made a superb job of putting the book together - Fiona, Ali, Jennifer and Lin and finally thanks to Simon Whitmore for the wonderful photography, taken at Rosemary Vernon's lovely house in Surrey, and to designer Lisa Forrester, who have made this such a beautiful book.

The publishers and author would like to thank William, Hannah, Lucy and Kate.

about the author

Dorothy Wood is a talented and prolific craft maker and author. Since completing a course in Advanced Embroidery and Textiles at Goldsmith's College, London, she has written twelve craft books, and contributed to another twenty, on all kinds of subjects. Dorothy also contributes to several well-known craft magazines, including *Crafts Beautiful*. Dorothy lives in the small village of Osgathorpe, Leicestershire, UK.

index